THE
Workplace
Skills

PRESENTATION GUIDE

THE
Workplace Skills

PRESENTATION GUIDE

Laurie Cope Grand

John Wiley & Sons, Inc.
New York • Chichester • Weinheim • Brisbane • Singapore • Toronto

---

Note about Photocopy Rights

The publisher grants purchasers permission to reproduce handouts from this book for professional use with their clients.

ISBN 0-471-37446-6

Printed in the United States of America.

10 9 8 7 6 5 4 3 2 1

For Lisa Ann Grand

Contents

Contents

Contents

Chapter 10.   Manage Your Stress 10.1

Chapter 11.   How to Create a Positive Work Environment 11.1

Chapter 12.   Managing Conflict at Work 12.1

Chapter 13.   The Art of Effective Communication 13.1

Contents

About the Disk D.1

Introduction

What This Book Includes

The Workplace Skills Presentation Guide includes 10 presentations for you to use to market your counseling practice. Each title includes a detailed presenter's outline, a list of reading material for your reference when you are preparing for a presentation, a sample marketing letter, and a press release.

Customize to Meet Your Audience's Needs

You may wish to mix and match the *content* of the presentation outlines and the handouts to meet the specific needs of various audiences. You may also want to change the *name* of your presentations to more exactly fit the needs and interests of your audiences. For example, "Does Your Company Need Family Therapy?" could be called "Build a Stronger Work Team" when presented to Chamber of Commerce members. "Manage Your Stress" could be renamed "Keep Holiday Stress under Control" when presented to store managers at the local mall.

Participant Handouts

Each topic includes a set of participant handouts. You may remove them from this book and reproduce them or use the files on the enclosed disk to edit and print them. Be creative: Mix and match the topics and alter the handouts to fit your personality and to meet the needs of your audience.

Visual Aids

Visuals always add value to a presentation. I recommend that you purchase a blank flip-chart pad and some markers from an office supply store and prepare posters before your presentation.

Videos

Most of the presentations include references to short scenes from popular movies that many of your participants may have seen. Including these videos as examples of various points in your presentations is a way to make them more interesting. If you can think of other scenes to add or use instead of the examples provided, feel free to substitute them.

Some videos may require that you obtain the permission of the copyright holder before you use them in certain types of presentations. Find out what the requirements are and obtain the necessary permission.

Be sure to check with the facility where you are giving your presentation to be sure they have a working VCR (in VHS format) and monitor. If they don't, consider bringing your own equipment.

THE
Workplace
Skills

PRESENTATION GUIDE

Chapter 1

How to Build Your Practice with Presentations

Research Your Audience

First, *decide whom you want to market your services to.* The 10 workshops in this collection contain information relevant to just about every business and organization. Any organized group has people who need to know how to create a positive work environment, manage conflict and stress, and so on, and they need these skills.

There are many places to *look for names and addresses of businesses* to offer your services to. Look through the Yellow Pages and the Chamber of Commerce Community Guide. If you live in an urban area, many cities have weekly business publications such as *Crain's Chicago Business* and *The Los Angeles Business Journal.* They often publish annual listings of businesses that may even include names of people to contact. The publication may also be available on disk, making it easy to convert to a mailing list.

Search the Internet for names and addresses of contacts. Many cities and towns publish lists of local businesses and organizations on their web sites. If you don't know where to begin, go to a search engine like Yahoo! or Lycos (www.yahoo.com or www.lycos.com) and type in the name of your city or town.

Design a brochure. Please see the sample brochure, Exhibit 1.1. It was designed with Microsoft Publisher 2000 and may be printed on paper purchased from an office supply store or from a company such as PaperDirect. They offer hundreds of beautiful styles. Call 1-800-A-PAPERS or visit www.paperdirect.com to request a catalog.

In your brochure, describe the series of workshops and offer to present them as a *community service.* Send the brochure to every business and civic organization in your area. Follow up with a phone call.

Another option is to *design a separate flyer* for each of the workshops in your series. Send them one at a time, once every six or eight weeks, to local businesses and civic groups. Send them to every kind of business in your area—plumbers, hardware stores, hospitals, doctors' offices, the veterinarian, the realtors. They all need the skills addressed in these workshops.

Design a workbook based on the handouts. Send them to local businesses and groups along with a brochure or flyer offering your services as a presenter.

Offer to speak on a local *radio or television show* about any of the topics. Put together a media kit with your glossy photo and bio, along with an outline of what you'd like to talk about.

Send your brochure and a letter to the managers of local bookstores. Offer to *conduct free workshops* during the spring or fall months at the bookstores or at your office. In your letter, request a meeting with each store manager. At the meeting, discuss your plan. Offer to supply the brochures or flyers and request that they be stacked at the wrap desk or by the front door. Visit the stores regularly to make sure there is a supply of the flyers available for customers to take.

If you are planning to offer your workshops for free, you may want to consider *asking the company to pay for the cost of copying* and packaging your handouts.

Offer to *conduct the "Balancing Work and Family" workshops* at the local pediatrician's office. Send a cover letter and flyer or brochure to every pediatrician in your area and follow up with a phone call.

Think about other logical places to offer the "Balancing Work and Family" workshops. Here are a few ideas: any kind of school, churches and temples, business groups such as Business and Professional Women, the Chamber of Commerce, LEADS, and so on.

If you are new to your Chamber of Commerce and want to stand out, consider offering your workshops to the *Chamber of Commerce office staff.* Send your materials to the Chamber president and follow up with a phone call.

Consider working with a partner, especially if you are anxious about speaking before groups. Having another therapist as a partner to co-lead your workshops with you will most likely considerably lessen your anxiety level. He or she can also help you brainstorm ways to market the workshops and participate in developing, distributing, and *paying for* the marketing materials.

Maximize your impact with *good timing.* Anticipate when people are likely to be preoccupied and are more likely to toss your offers in the wastebasket. For example, don't approach your local retailers between November 1 and mid-January. Stay away from anything to do with accounting from February through April. The pediatrician offices are usually swamped in August and September.

Offer to present your workshops through a *local office supply store* like Staples or Office Depot. These stores sometimes offer workshops to the public on business-related subjects, and yours would be a perfect addition. Prepare a sample flyer and ask for an appointment with the store manager.

When a company asks you to present your workshop on site, *meet with the senior management representatives* and discuss their needs. Prepare a list of questions to ask before you go. Find out which workshops they are interested in and why. Ask them what their goals are and what results they would like to see after the workshops.

Before you present an in-company workshop, ask your contact at the company if you can assess the needs of the employees who will be attending. *Develop a questionnaire* that will help you gather relevant information to help you prepare your presentation.

Ask to *meet with small groups of employees* to learn more about the company and the issues that people are concerned about. This information will help you focus your presentation on issues that people care about and avoid less relevant issues.

Spend some time *visiting the company* as a customer, if possible. If it is a public place like a store, shop there a few times and see how it feels to be a customer. These visits will help you learn more about the climate and culture.

Find out if the company has an *employee newsletter.* If they do, offer to write a short article that's related to your workshop. You are free to use the text of your outlines and handouts, as long as you give credit to the original sources.

Use the information in the outlines to *write a series of articles* for your local newspaper, Chamber of Commerce newsletter, or business journal.

Advertise. Arrange to present the workshops and run ads in your local paper. Include your picture and a reference to your upcoming workshop.

Write a *press release* about your event and send it with your glossy publicity photo to every local media outlet. Make sure you have the permission of your contact at the company where you are making your presentation. There is a sample (see Exhibit 1.2), and each presentation outline has wording for a press release.

Package your handouts to look professional and impressive. You want people to say "wow!" when they see them. Spend the money to package them in a nice folder and place your business card in each one. Avery makes a nice folder—you can print your own design on the cover, using your own printer. They are somewhat expensive, but remember that you want to make a strong impression.

Following Up Your Presentation

Prepare an *evaluation form* for participants to complete after your presentation. It can be as simple as Exhibit 1.3. Ask people to complete it and leave it by the door as they exit. It will provide you with useful feedback for next time. If the feedback is favorable, you can use it to market future presentations. If it's not so favorable, just learn from it. There will always be people who like you and people who don't.

The day after your workshop, send a handwritten *thank-you note* to your contact at the company.

Exhibit 1.1   A Sample Brochure

Four Community Service Workshops

Would your employees value a presentation on one of these topics? Please call *Your Name* to schedule your workshop.

All workshops are offered at no charge as a service to members of the *Your Town* business community.

Presented by
Your Name,
Licensed Counselor in
Your Town

(555) 555-1234
www.yourwebsite.com

Your employees will work together even better when they learn these skills:

- Managing Emotions in the Workplace

- How to Create a Positive Work Environment

- Balancing Work and Family

- How to Give Constructive Performance Feedback

Workshops for the Workplace

Build new skills to help your team work together even better

Presented by
Your Name,
Licensed Counselor
in *Your Town*

(555) 555-1234
www.yourwebsite.com

Place
your photo
here

Managing Emotions in the Workplace

Based on Daniel Goleman's book *Emotional Intelligence at Work,* this workshop helps participants learn how to:

- Recognize how their emotions affect their work behavior and performance.
- Assess their own emotional strengths and limitations.
- Assess work experiences and identify areas where they wish to do things differently.
- Respond to challenging work situations with appropriate empathy and listening skills.

Participants learn these behaviors through a combination of lecture, analysis of popular movies, case studies, and practice exercises.

Presented to the *Your Town* business community by *Your Name,* Licensed Counselor

To learn about other services, visit www.yourwebsite.com

How to Create a Positive Work Environment

We have all worked in places where we grew to hate getting up in the morning, and a few of us have had the pleasure of working for a boss who made us feel like we could do anything. Through lecture, group discussion, practice exercises, and analysis of popular movies, participants will learn specific ways to make their workplace a more positive place by motivating and reinforcing their coworkers.

Other Workshop Titles

The following workshops are also available for your business team: Career Crash, Does Your Company Need Family Therapy, Take Charge of Your Life: Plan Your Best Year Yet, Manage Your Stress, Managing Conflict at Work, and The Art of Effective Communication. Let's talk about how we can customize a workshop to meet the needs of your work group.

To schedule a workshop for your company, call **(555) 555-1234**

Balancing Work and Family

In the aftermath of the downsized 1990s, most people report heavier workloads and increased expectations at work. It is becoming more and more difficult for many people to meet the obligations of both work and home. Through a series of exercises and group discussions, participants evaluate their own work/family situations, learning skills to simplify life and regain balance.

How to Give Constructive Performance Feedback

An important part of being a manager is giving employees constructive, specific feedback about their job performance. Unfortunately, many employees never know whether they are doing their jobs properly because feedback is communicated ineffectively. In this workshop, participants will learn five basic steps of giving an employee specific performance feedback. Skills will be developed through lecture, demonstration, and a variety of practice exercises.

Exhibit 1.2   A Sample Press Release

For Immediate Release

Sandy Bonds
233 Kilpatrick St.
Olympia, NY 10278
555/555-0405

CONTACT: Sandy Bonds

"Managing People in the Workplace" Series
Presented by Local Therapist

Olympia, NY—February 22, 20XX—Sandy Bonds, M.A., is presenting a
series of workshops for businesspeople in the greater Olympia area. The
series will meet on Tuesdays from 7 to 9 P.M. starting on March 13. All
four sessions will be held at the Olympia Counseling Center on Kilpatrick
Avenue. The sessions are limited to 20 participants and are being presented
as a public service.

"Getting along well with people is the most important set of skills in every
business today," says Ms. Bonds. "In college, most people learn the technical skills they need to get them in the door at a company, but it's the ability
to get along with people that enables a person to become an effective team
leader." The series of four workshops includes "Managing Emotions in the
Workplace," "How to Create a Positive Work Environment," "How to Give
Constructive Feedback," and "Balancing Work and Family." Ms. Bonds
offers the workshops at the Olympia Counseling Center as well as for individual companies.

Ms. Bonds has been a licensed marriage and family therapist in New York
since 1985. She is also the former director of personnel for a Long Island
insurance company. To make a reservation or for more information, call the
Olympia Counseling Center at (555) 555-0405.

# # # #

Exhibit 1.3   A Sample Workshop Evaluation Form

Workshop Evaluation Form

Thank you for your comments about today's workshop. Please answer the following questions and leave this form at the door.

1. What did you like best about today's workshop?

2. What did you learn?

3. What did you like least?

4. What suggestions do you have for future workshops?

Thank you for your comments and suggestions.

Chapter 2

Presentation Pointers

Chapter 2

Many people are uncomfortable with the idea of speaking before a group. Here are some ways you can prepare yourself to give a professional, successful presentation.

1. *Learn about your audience and their needs.*

Who is your audience?

Ask your contact in the organization to describe who will be in the audience. Some questions to ask include:

- What are the audience members likely to know about you and your subject?

- How are they likely to feel about being there?

- What do they already know about your topic?

- What are their views about psychotherapy and psychotherapists?

- What special needs do they have?

What is the purpose of meeting?

Some questions to ask about the meeting include:

- Why is this group meeting?

- What is the occasion? Is this a regular weekly or monthly meeting, and is a speaker usually invited?

- What kinds of speakers have made presentations in the past?

How formal is the occasion?

- Will this be a small group gathered around a table or a large group (50 or more) sitting auditorium-style in rows of seats?

- How well do the participants know one another? Are they used to some kind of interaction and participation or are they expecting a lecture?

- Will there be a lectern, microphone, and audiovisual equipment?

- If this is a small group, is there an easel and flip-chart pad available?

What is the context of your presentation?

- Are you the only speaker, perhaps the featured speaker at a luncheon meeting, or are you one of several?

- How does your topic relate to the other subjects being discussed before and after your presentation?

How long should you speak?

- Find out the total amount of time available.

- Will there be one or more breaks?

- Is time for questions and answers included?

At what time of day will you speak?

- If you are scheduled to speak during a meal, expect audience members to be distracted.

- If you are speaking after a meal, build some exercises and participation into your presentation to avoid having people drift off to sleep.

2. *Arrange the meeting room.*

Arrange the seating. If at all possible before your presentation, arrange the meeting room to enable people to see and hear you easily. (Refer to Exhibit 2.1.) Choose an arrangement that fits the purpose of the meeting. For example:

- Auditorium-style seating works best for large groups (more than 50) and lectures.

- Tables of 6 to 10 people are appropriate when participants will be writing and interacting with each other.

- Rows of chairs and tables with a center aisle enable people to take notes and allow the speaker to walk into the audience.

Will you use a lectern?

- A lectern can be comforting if you are nervous. It gives you something to hide behind and a place to put your notes.

- Standing next to the lectern or stepping away from it makes you more accessible to the audience.

- Unless you are speaking to a very small group, plan to stand during your presentation. Speaking while seated makes you appear much less powerful.

3. *Prepare appropriate visual aids.*

Prepare flip charts and posters. It is always more interesting for the audience when you provide something for them to look at. Posters of your key points are a very effective way to add interest and clarity to your presentation.

- An inexpensive idea is to make posters of your key points on a newsprint flip-chart pad. Prepare this ahead of time and rehearse your presentation using the flip chart. Make sure the printing is large enough for people in the back of the room to see.

- Inexpensive pads may be purchased at office supply stores.

- Another advantage of having visuals prepared ahead of time is that it makes your key points easier to remember.

- You can rely on the information on your flip chart to guide you as you make your presentation.

- You can also write a few more key ideas lightly in pencil as reminders while you speak. Knowing this information is there for you helps reduce the jitters.

Prepare slides. You may have slides made for a professional touch.

- Expect each slide to cost several dollars, and allow enough time to have them made.

- If you decide to use slides, practice using the equipment before the audience enters the room.

2.3

- If you plan to use the remote control, try it out before your presentation to be sure it works properly.

- Stay away from the screen as you are speaking, or you will block the audience's view. You will also be lit up along with the screen, and you may look a bit strange.

Prepare transparencies.   Transparencies are another inexpensive yet professional way to provide information visually.

- Place each transparency in a cardboard frame (which you can purchase inexpensively at office supply stores). Transparencies tend to stick together from static electricity, and the frame prevents this.

- Turn off the transparency machine when you switch to the next visual. Turn it back on when you've placed the next transparency on it. Leaving the machine on with no transparency can feel blinding to the audience.

- Stay away from the screen as you are speaking, or you will block the audience's view. You will also be lit up along with the screen, and you may look a bit strange.

4. *Prepare your presentation.*

Develop the outline and content.

- Your presentation should have a beginning, a middle, and an end.

- Include as many examples as you can think of—at least one for each point. Examples and illustrations bring your presentation to life and make it more interesting.

- Develop about 25 percent more content than you think you'll need. Then you won't have to worry about running out of things to say.

- If possible, make your presentation interactive. Build in a few exercises for people to do, either individually or in small groups.

- Prepare questions to ask the participants throughout your presentation. Note a few answers to each question, in case no one responds.

Design the handouts.

- Handouts should be written in simple language with plenty of white space.

- Include your name and phone number on your handouts.

- Always credit your sources.

- Prepare more handouts than you think you'll need.

Gather the supplies.   Pack the following supplies for your presentation:

- Your outline
- Participant handouts
- Markers

- Masking tape
- Business cards
- Your practice brochure
- Visual aids (slides, transparencies, or posters)

Optional supplies include:

- Videos (cued to the correct scene)
- Audiotapes or CDs
- Cassette or CD player

5. *Rehearse your presentation.*

Visit the meeting room. If it's possible to visit the room where your presentation will be held, doing so will accomplish a number of things.

- You will feel more confident and calm before your meeting when you can visualize the setting. The unknown is always more intimidating than what is known.

- Seeing the room will enable you to plan for possible contingencies that you may not otherwise have known about. For example, the room may be much larger or much smaller than you expected.

Videotape yourself.

- If you have access to a video camera, by all means use it to practice your presentation. There is nothing like video feedback to show you what you do well and where you could improve.

- Be sure to videotape yourself a second time after you've practiced a few more times. You'll see improvements and it will help your confidence.

Audiotape yourself and use the tape to practice.

- Audiotaping yourself as you practice is useful for the same reasons listed for videotaping.

- A second use of a practice audiotape is to play it in your car during the days before your presentation. It will help you memorize the key points of your talk as well.

Practice using the equipment. You have probably attended a seminar or workshop where the presenter fumbled with the VCR or microphones and became pretty embarrassed. Don't make the same mistake. It takes only a few minutes to practice using the equipment that's part of your presentation, even if it's as simple as a transparency projector.

6. *During the presentation.*

Introduce yourself. Unless you're being introduced by someone else, be sure to state your name and what you do before you do anything else. It may seem obvious, but speakers have been known to omit this important piece of information.

Repeat questions.

Unless your meeting room is fairly small, it's courteous to repeat questions from people in the audience before you answer. Don't assume everyone heard every question.

Smile.

Even though you may be nervous, don't forget to smile. People want you to succeed. They usually are focusing much less attention on you than you think, and they usually just assume you know what you are talking about.

Look at one person at a time.

You will build the best rapport with your audience if you look at their faces and talk to them as individuals.

Breathe.

You will stay calmer if you remember to breathe.

Slow down.

If possible, have an ally in the audience who can signal you if you start talking too fast.

Answer questions.

Always set aside some time to find out what questions people have. Ask for questions with an open-ended question such as, "What questions do you have?" Then be silent and allow people time to think and respond.

Say thank you.

Always conclude your presentation by thanking the audience for their time and attention.

Exhibit 2.1   Types of Seating Arrangements

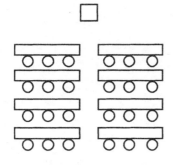

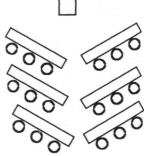

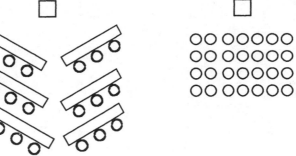

**Seminar
Arrangement
with Tables**

Effective seating for a fairly
large group who will be taking
notes; this is a very comfortable way to seat people for an
all-day workshop where they
will need to spread out.

**V-Shape with
Tables**

Effective seating for a fairly
large group who will be taking
notes; the V-shape enables the
speaker to step into the audience and establish closer contact than with auditorium-style
seating.

Auditorium

An effective arrangement for
very large groups; works well
for a lecture with minimal
interaction.

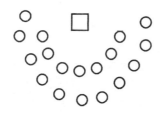

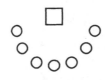

Double Semicircle

Enables the speaker to be
closer to the audience members; allows more intimacy.

Semicircle

Provides a more intimate setting for a small group.

Chapter 3

12 Tips for Marketing Your Practice

Why Should You Market Your Practice?

Let's talk about why marketing is a critical skill for a successful counseling or psychotherapy practice.

1. *To build your business.* The first reason to market is the most obvious: Most therapists in private practice want more clients. Marketing is a way to find those clients and get them to call you.
2. *To let people know you exist.* Marketing is a series of activities that will tell the people in your marketplace that you exist. Without marketing, how will people find out about you? There will always be a few therapists who will tell you they just opened their doors and people started calling, but these are the exceptions. The rest of us need to spend at least 50 percent of our time marketing.
3. *To have a road map.* When you design and implement a marketing campaign, you create a road map for yourself and your business. It gives you a sense of direction and something to measure results against. This gives most businesspeople a feeling of security and satisfaction, which is lacking when there is no plan.
4. *To understand where your business comes from* so you can get more. A marketing program includes certain elements that all fit together. You will analyze your market, set goals, implement your plans, and measure the results of your efforts. As you begin to see results, you will understand what actions produced those results. You will know what actions to repeat to get more results. You will also know what actions failed to produce results, and you will not want to repeat them.

Now let's look at a few tips that should give you some direction in your marketing efforts.

Marketing Tip #1: Analyze the Marketplace

Can you imagine starting a new business without first understanding who lives in the area surrounding it? It's amazing, but many therapists do just that when they set up their first practice. Let's look at what such an analysis involves and why it's a crucial step.

Define your marketplace in terms of:

1. *Competition.* One important part of your market analysis is taking a look at the competition. Who else is practicing in your area? You will want to find out the following information:

    - How many other therapists are there within a 2- to 5-mile radius?
    - What licenses do these therapists hold? How many of each type of license?

- What can you learn about the practice specialties of these competitors?
- What kinds of marketing are your competitors doing?
- How visible are they? Are they more than just listings in the Yellow Pages?

It's a good idea to get in your car and take a drive. See what office buildings your competitors are located in. Make notes. Mark their locations on a map. See where they cluster. What opportunities do you see?

2. *Demographics.* This data includes facts about the people who live in your area. It includes things like:

- Average age
- Income
- Education
- Occupation
- Marital status
- Gender
- Family size
- Percentage who are homeowners
- Average home price

This information can be found at places such as the following:

- The Chamber of Commerce
- The public library (ask the librarian)
- Local business publications
- Real estate offices

This information is important, especially when you are deciding where to open a practice. Many people consider psychotherapy to be an expensive service, and demographic factors will help you decide the most favorable locations to open such a business. It will also help you decide which specialty areas to market, based on the population living in your market area.

3. *Trends.* Current trends are important to consider when you are designing a marketing plan for your practice. Examples of trends are:

- More young families moving in
- Senior citizen population expanding
- Large companies expanding or downsizing
- Mergers and closings
- More of certain ethnic groups moving in
- Recent disasters (earthquakes, floods, hurricanes, tornadoes, etc.) that have impacted the economy as well as people's psyches

You can learn about such trends in the following ways:

- Read the paper.
- Surf the Internet.
- Walk through the mall or down the street.
- Watch TV news shows.

Marketing Tip #2:
Know Your Competition

Understanding your competition is a very important element of your success. First, look in the Yellow Pages and other listings and be sure you understand who is out there vying for the same clients you are. Then you have to get creative. You want to find out what those competitors of yours are really like.

- How do they do business?
- How do they treat clients?
- What are their offices like?

One way to do this is to go "therapist shopping." It's a bit like being a mystery shopper in a department store. Choose a few therapists whom you'd like to know more about. Call their offices and ask if you can meet with them. Say you're doing a survey of the market area and you want to get to know the other practitioners. Make a list of questions you'd like to ask, such as:

- Hours of availability
- How they work with clients
- Areas of specialty
- Fees

If possible, visit each therapist. Note how you feel as you walk into the office building, the waiting room, and the therapy room. How might a client feel? What impression do you get as you meet with each person? What do you think he or she does particularly well?

Identify ways your practice is superior or unique. After you've met with a few of your competitors, make a list of what you've learned. What do most therapists do especially well? What opportunities do you see to excel? Evaluate your findings in terms of the following factors:

- How long licensed?
- Any special training?
- Specialty areas?
- Affordable fees?
- Comfortable, nonintimidating office?
- Feeling of safety in the parking lot and building?
- Conveys a feeling of confidence?
- Conveys a feeling of warmth?
- Office feels private?
- Confidential atmosphere; files are locked and conversations are private?

Find new ways to create more value for your clients. Consider the practice elements listed in this section. Think of the other therapists in your market area, and make a list of at least five ways you could create more value today for your clients.

Marketing Tip #3:
Know What Your Clients Value

In *The Guerrilla Marketing Handbook* (a must-read, along with the entire Guerrilla Marketing series), Jay Conrad Levinson and Seth Godin write that one key to success in your practice is to deliver more than the customer expects. They write, "Act on the knowledge that customers value attention, dependability, promptness, and competence" (page 348).

Compare yourself to your competition in terms of these four elements—attention, dependability, promptness, and competence—and find five ways to create more value for your clients. You will soon have more clients.

Here are a few things to consider:

1. *Concrete aspects of your service.* This includes things like the following:

   - The length of your sessions
   - Your fee
   - Insurance reimbursement; participation in managed care programs
   - How much information you provide your clients
   - What other services you offer besides counseling
   - What kinds of clients and issues you work well with

   You have made decisions about each of these aspects of your service. Do your decisions match what your clients value?

2. *Office location.* Think about the following:

   - How easy is the office to find?
   - Is there plenty of parking? Is it free?
   - Does it feel safe in the daytime and at night?
   - Is it accessible to people with disabilities?
   - Is it clean?
   - Is it comfortable and friendly?
   - Does it convey a professional feeling?

   Again, you have made decisions about each of these aspects of your service. Do your decisions match what your clients value?

3. *Time* is an important part of your service. Think about the following, and add your own items to the list.

   - How long are your sessions? Have you started seeing clients for less time at the same fee? How do you think the clients feel about this? What would happen if you did the opposite—perhaps offer 90-minute sessions at the original fee? Remember, those who give the client more than he or she expects will be the winners in this competitive climate.
   - Are you available when your clients are? Are you rigidly seeing clients once each week, or are you willing to be flexible and try new arrangements? What about seeing them every other week

with a 10-minute telephone touch base in between? It would mean one less trip to your office for your busy clients. Many of them might appreciate it.

- How quickly do you work? Are you willing to embrace the current methods of doing therapy and spend less time with each client? Have you asked your clients what they prefer?

4. *Convenience.* How easy do you make it for your clients to get what they need and want from you? Are there unnecessary barriers that may have gone unnoticed and that could be eliminated?

   For example: Therapist Gilda's only available hours are on Tuesdays and Saturdays. She works for a "therapy mill" (a large group practice) and is one of about 20 therapists on the staff. The only way for clients to reach her is through the practice, and they must always leave a message. There are no voice mail and no pager. The frustration created by this lack of availability is enormous. And so are the opportunities for the competition!

What are your own examples of how you could create more value for your clients than the competition does?

Marketing Tip #4: Know What Makes You Unique

Why is it so important to stand out from the crowd? To give clients a reason to choose you instead of the many other therapists available—or instead of choosing the option of "do-it-yourself" therapy.

Always ask yourself, "Why would a client choose me?" Make a list of at least five ways that you are different from almost everyone else. Don't worry if they don't seem to relate to the business of psychotherapy. Here are some examples:

- Anne was born in Israel and speaks fluent Hebrew.
- Krystal spent 15 years as an executive recruiter before becoming a therapist.
- Steve is a cancer survivor.
- Susan is a registered dietician and licensed psychologist.
- Belinda is an adoptive parent.

Stress your unique points in every marketing effort. The point, of course, is to find several ways in which you are different from almost every other therapist—and emphasize those differences in your marketing campaign. Here is how the five therapists you just read about stressed their differences in their practices:

- Anne markets her counseling services to Israeli immigrants. She conducts many of her sessions in Hebrew.
- Krystal specializes in career counseling and offers a support group for survivors of corporate downsizing.
- Steve specializes in working with the families of people with serious illnesses.

- Susan specializes in working with clients with eating disorders.
- Belinda offers support groups for prospective adoptive parents.

Marketing Tip #5: Emphasize the Benefits of Your Services

To help you differentiate your counseling services from those of your competitors, you must learn to spell out the features and benefits. The first step is to define your service. Second, list the features your counseling service offers that are different from the services your competitors offer. Then, for each feature, identify the benefits of your service. Benefits answer the question, "Why is this important to me?"

Stress these benefits in all of your marketing efforts. Here is another way of looking at benefits: They answer the question, "How does my service make my client's life better?"

Marketing Tip #6: See Yourself from the Client's Perspective

What impression do you make? Being competitive means staying aware of how you come across to your clients, especially in first impressions.

If you have recently shopped for a therapist for yourself or for a family member, the experience may have been an eye-opener. Chances are, it reminded you that we must always be aware of how we come across to our clients—in so many ways.

1. *Through your written communications.* Be aware that your written communications—your business stationery, Yellow Pages ad, other ads, and so on—create an impression with potential clients. Do yours help you stand out from the crowd, or do they look like everyone else's?

   Look at your business cards. How are they similar to the business cards of other therapists? How are they different? What impact is each likely to make on a prospective client? The purpose here is not to be judgmental, but to learn about what makes an impact.

2. *During the first phone contact.* Recently, when looking for a therapist, a client left a message requesting a return call to discuss starting therapy. When the therapist called back, it was obvious that she was holding a baby as she talked on the phone. The client could hear the baby gurgling in the background and the therapist even had to excuse herself once to shift the baby to another position.

   What is wrong with this therapist's behavior on the phone, and how is this related to marketing?

- The behavior is unprofessional and not businesslike.
- A client in distress may be distracted or upset by hearing a baby in the background.
- The therapist had no knowledge about this client. Consider the possibility that this client is infertile or has other issues that would make her especially sensitive to hearing a baby.

3. *In your waiting room.* A large, busy practice specializing in children's issues has a waiting room that is almost always overflowing with families. It is very noisy and chaotic. The magazines are strewn about and their covers are torn. This practice is in a fairly small town, so clients get the feeling that their problems are on public view. They often see other families from their school coming and going.

   The office staff members of this practice sit in a room next to the waiting room and make telephone calls to clients and other professionals within the hearing of the waiting clients. Names and medications are freely mentioned with no attempt at privacy.

   Aside from the ethical violations, what is wrong with this picture—from a *customer service* point of view?

   - The client feels a lack of privacy.
   - The chaotic waiting room adds to clients' anxiety.
   - When overhearing the staff discussing other clients, waiting clients wonder how their own information is overheard.

4. *At the first meeting.* At a busy nonprofit counseling center, new clients coming for the first visit (called an *intake,* not a particularly customer-friendly term) are handed a clipboard with several pages of forms to fill out. The intake therapist rattles off a long series of questions and takes notes. What impression do you suppose this might make on the client?

   While information gathering is necessary, especially in the beginning, what negative impression might it create? How might this impression be softened? Be aware of the tendency to ask questions in a rote manner. Acknowledge to the client the possible negative feeling created by such questions. Perhaps you can think of a few more examples of ways therapists might create a negative impression during the first session.

Marketing Tip #7: Identify Your Target Client

You may have heard the marketing term *target market.* Have you identified yours? Let's find out how this will help you build a strong practice. Most therapists market their services to two groups:

- People who will be their clients
- People or groups who will refer clients to the practice

This is an important distinction. Be sure to identify who belongs in each of these categories for your practice and include them both in your marketing strategy. For example:

Target clients: People who are infertile
Referral sources: Reproductive endocrinologists

How do people choose a therapist? Here are a few typical ways:

- Consult a Yellow Pages ad.
- Ask their doctor or clergy.
- Ask the school psychologist.
- Ask a friend or relative.
- Attend a seminar or workshop given by a therapist.
- Consult a managed care list.

Most referrals are based on someone's knowledge about the therapist. Therefore, it is important that you:

- Make contact with as many potential referrers as you can—by networking.
- Make it as easy as possible for people to refer to you—by networking.
- Make it as easy as possible for potential clients to choose you—by being visible and active in your community.

Since the most important element in the choice of a therapist is trust, your key task is to make yourself as accessible as possible. What kinds of things would add to your accessibility? You could do things like these:

- Include your photo in your advertisements (Yellow Pages, newspaper, flyers, etc.).
- Participate in numerous networking events, for as long as you are in business.
- Offer to speak to groups.
- Give free seminars and events at your office or in hotel meeting rooms.

Marketing Tip #8:
Market to Your Target Client

A target client has certain specific traits, such as their demographic profile, geographic location, and type of lifestyle. Target marketing is different from general marketing in that you identify a specific segment or niche and design all of your marketing activities to appeal to clients belonging to that group. Examples of target clients include:

- Upper middle class, married, $75K income and above, living in zip code 91107, no children, age 30 to 39
- Middle class, divorced, single parents, $20K to $40K income, living in zip codes 91405 to 91407, age 25 to 40

How might the services for these two groups be different? Here are some possible ways:

- The first group would be most interested in couples groups, marital therapy, career issues, and workshops on personal growth issues.

- The second group would be interested in a workshop on survival skills for single parents, evening availability, family therapy, and brief therapy.

In *Rocking the Ages: The Yankelovich Report on Generational Marketing* (noted in the Resource List at the end of this chapter), authors J. Walker Smith and Ann Clurman describe how effective marketing campaigns can be designed based on understanding the generation to which the target client belongs: Generation X, the Baby Boomers, and what the authors call the Matures. The authors state that the values, preferences, and behaviors of consumers can be understood by recognizing "three distinct elements: 1) life stage, 2) current social and economic conditions, and 3) formative cohort experiences." If you identify the generation of your target clients, you can better target your services to meet their needs and values.

Set your fees based on this client. When setting your fees, you should consider the following factors:

- What your competitors are charging
- What your clients consider a reasonable amount
- Trends in your area and in your profession
- Your target client

Fees are difficult to price because your service is intangible. Some experts say that those who purchase services see price as an indicator of quality, so a lower fee has a negative impact on how potential clients might see you.

In *The Guerrilla Marketing Handbook* (noted in the Resource List at the end of this chapter), Levinson and Godin write, "When a customer tells you that your price is too high, what he's really saying is, that you don't give enough value for what you're charging. Time and time again, aggressive businesses have shown that people will pay for quality and service. . . . Your price is rarely the problem. Worry instead about benefits, positioning, and service" (page 306).

Avoid the temptation to lose your focus. Building a successful practice takes a few years. When results are lacking, it is tempting to blame your marketing campaign and think about trying something different. If your program is based on a well-thought-out analysis, however, changing tracks may be the wrong move. It will certainly be confusing to your colleagues and referral sources.

Try the following instead:

- Talk it over with someone who can advise you.
- Consider making minor adjustments to your plan before you make any radical changes.
- Ask a few trusted friends or colleagues to help you brainstorm ways to get your business moving.

Marketing Tip #9: Develop a Marketing Plan and Short-Term Objectives

It is critical to write your plan down and refer to it often. You need both a long-range plan covering the next one to three years and short-term objectives for the coming 6 to 12 months.

Objectives are effective only if they are written in language that is

- Specific
- Concrete
- Measurable

Update your objectives regularly. Once you've developed a killer set of objectives, don't stick them in the drawer and forget about them. Do just the opposite: Put them to work, and keep them up to date.

- Put them on your bulletin board right next to your desk.
- Make an action calendar with subgoals and checkoff lists.
- Reward yourself when you accomplish what you set out to do.

Marketing Tip #10: Design a Promotional Strategy

A promotional strategy is a combination of activities designed to attract people's attention and get them to call for an appointment. How will people hear about you?

A promotional strategy is necessary because you need to have a plan for how people will find out about you. Just hanging out your shingle and hoping the phone will ring is not a strategy. Neither is "if I build it, they will come." A strategy is a set of actions designed to accomplish a specific goal.

Promotions include things like advertisements, public relations, and sales promotions. When deciding whether to advertise, consider your target market and special services you've developed for them. Choose the medium your target client is most likely to read.

Generate publicity by staging events such as your own seminars and workshops, and offering to speak to community groups. Develop a mailing list of media outlets—every one you can think of—and regularly send them press releases announcing your events and programs. *Guerrilla P.R.* by Michael Levine (see Resource List) is an excellent resource.

A random promotional strategy will produce random results at best. Most likely, such a strategy will produce no results at all.

Marketing Tip #11: Measure the Results of Your Efforts

This tip may seem like an obvious one, but it is one of the most important points of this workshop. Let's look at why.

Therapist Sheila decides to run a few ads to get her practice going. In Week 1, she spends $78 to run a small but tasteful ad in the local paper. No calls. She thinks, I must need more time. So she spends another $78 on an ad during the second week. One call, but no appointment was scheduled. In Week 3, she decides that her ad isn't big enough. So she spends $132 for a larger ad. Again, one call, but no appointment. And in Week 4, she tries one more time. She just can't believe that the ads didn't produce anything. But she can't resist trying again. She thinks, maybe repetition is the key. After all, she sees so many other businesses with similar ads in the same paper, week after week. Maybe it takes a few months to make people notice me.

After 10 weeks, Sheila is out of money. What did she get for her ads? Three calls, and one scheduled a consultation. The client no-showed, by the way!

Interestingly, other therapists in town saw Sheila's ads. After a few weeks, they thought, this Sheila must be very successful if she can afford all of this advertising!

Analyze the Costs and Results of Each Marketing Activity

Let's assume that Sheila did have a marketing plan. She gave herself four weeks of ads at $78 per week. She saw that for the ads to pay off, she would need to produce at least $4 \times \$78$, or $312, worth of business to break even. If her hourly fee was $80, she would need to see about four clients.

Do More of What Produces Results

The 80/20 rule, which is also known as the Pareto Principle, says that 80 percent of the results are produced by 20 percent of the resources. Applied to the business of psychotherapy, it means that 80 percent of the clients come from 20 percent of the referral sources. Know what your top 20 percent is and spend your energy making that grow.

Do Less of What Doesn't Produce Results

If an activity isn't producing results, stop doing it. Back to Sheila: We don't know enough about her ad to know why it didn't produce any clients. Perhaps the ad copy was the problem. Maybe the paper was the wrong place to advertise to attract the target client. Maybe Sheila never thought to target a client. But one thing is certain: If it wasn't working after the fourth week, she should have stopped what she was doing and tried something different.

Marketing Tip #12: Don't Give Up

Have you ever felt like giving up? It happens to all of us. It can be very discouraging, especially if you are a solo practitioner. But don't give up!

Allow enough time for your efforts to produce results. Building a successful practice takes a few years. There are no shortcuts. Expecting anything different is not being fair to yourself. If you are going to set out on this journey, you must be realistic in your estimate of how long it will take for success to come.

In another must-read, *Making It on Your Own,* Sarah and Paul Edwards devote an entire chapter to "Staying Up No Matter What Goes Down." Reading this book is like therapy for the discouraged private practitioner. The authors describe their own experiences with the fact that "success has a schedule of its own" (page 229).

Success is 99 percent persistence. I'm not sure who said it, but doesn't it seem true? Good things (success) come to those who persist.

What to Do When You Feel Like Quitting

Those who manage to hang on through the hard times when the phone isn't ringing and their only three clients cancelled must have a secret.

The following is a list of things you can do when you feel like quitting and going back to the career you left (because you hated it) before you became a therapist. Add your own ideas.

1. Spend some time with friends and colleagues who will tell you what a terrific therapist you are.
2. Reread your journal entries from the days when you were deciding to become a therapist.
3. Remember how much you disliked the career you had before you started graduate school.
4. Make a list of 20 reasons why you became a therapist.
5. Read the biographies of successful people. Note how most of them didn't become successful until they endured many failures and years of barely making it.
6. Write yourself a letter from the successful and satisfied professional you will be in five years and thank yourself for staying with it.

Keep your eye on your market. Remember, marketing goes on forever. It is an essential part of running your successful psychotherapy business. Never take your eye off your market.

Good luck. And luck *is* part of the equation.

Resource List

Beckwith, Harry. *Selling the Invisible: A Field Guide to Modern Marketing.* New York: Warner Books, 1997.

Edwards, Sarah and Paul. *Making It on Your Own: Surviving and Thriving On the Ups and Downs of Being Your Own Boss.* New York: Jeremy P. Tarcher, 1991.

Levine, Michael. *Guerrilla P.R.: How You Can Wage an Effective Publicity Campaign without Going Broke.* New York: HarperCollins, 1993.

Levinson, Jay, and Seth Godin. *The Guerrilla Marketing Handbook.* Boston: Houghton Mifflin, 1994.

Smith, J. Walker, and Ann Clurman. *Rocking the Ages: The Yankelovich Report on Generational Marketing.* New York: HarperCollins, 1997.

White, Sarah. *The Complete Idiot's Guide to Marketing Basics.* New York: Alpha Books, 1997.

Chapter 4

Increasing Emotional Intelligence in the Workplace

Presentation Synopsis

Based on Daniel Goleman's book *Working with Emotional Intelligence,* this workshop helps participants learn to:

- Recognize how their emotions affect their work behavior and performance.
- Assess their own emotional strengths and limitations.
- Assess work experiences and identify areas where they wish to do things differently.
- Respond to challenging work situations with appropriate empathy and listening skills.
- Negotiate and resolve disagreements.

Participants learn through a combination of lecture, discussion of scenes from popular movies, case studies, and practice exercises.

This presentation is based, in part, on information from the following books. I recommend that you review them as you prepare your presentation.

Goleman, Daniel. *Emotional Intelligence.* New York: Bantam Books, 1995.

Goleman, Daniel. *Working with Emotional Intelligence.* New York: Bantam Books, 1998.

Time Requirements

This presentation runs from 1½ hours to 2 hours, depending on the style of the presenter and the number of interactive activities used.

Clock symbol. This means that the information is included for a longer seminar or workshop. Omit these sections for a shorter presentation. If time is limited, another way to shorten your presentation is to share the information in lecture format. However, keep in mind that it is often harder to engage and maintain the audience's interest with pure lecture style. Unless you are a particularly dynamic speaker, you will probably want to keep at least a few of the exercises to enliven the presentation.

Video examples. It is suggested that you show scenes from the following videos during this workshop: *The Remains of the Day, Wall Street, Good Will Hunting,* and *As Good As It Gets.* Be sure to have the videos cued up before your participants arrive. Make certain you know how to operate all audiovisual equipment before you begin your presentation.

How to Use This Presentation

Possible Audiences	**Whom to Contact**
Businesspeople	Company presidents, human resources managers, or other executives; Chamber of Commerce, Rotary, and similar business groups
Adult education groups at churches and synagogues	Director of adult education programs
Women's civic and professional organizations	Director of educational programs

Sample Text for Marketing Letter, Brochure, or Postcard

Several recent researchers have concluded that the ability to get along well with people is more important than technical competence. Emotional Intelligence, the newest term for "people skills," is a set of competencies that can be learned. This workshop introduces participants to these important skills and can initiate a valuable learning process in your organization.

Based on Daniel Goleman's book *Emotional Intelligence at Work,* this workshop helps participants learn to recognize how their emotions affect their work behavior and performance, assess their own emotional strengths and limitations, assess work experiences and identify areas where they wish to do things differently, respond to challenging work situations with appropriate empathy and listening skills, and negotiate and resolve disagreements. This interactive workshop employs a combination of lecture, video examples, case studies, and practice exercises.

_____ is a licensed _____ in private practice in _____. S/he specializes in _____ and _____. Call _____ today to schedule your group's **free** workshop. (_____) _____-_____.

Sample Text for Press Release

_____ Presents "Increasing Emotional Intelligence in the Workplace"

_____ is presenting a **free** workshop on how to develop your ability to get along with people at work. The workshop is scheduled for _____, from _____ to _____ at _____.

The workshop is limited to _____ participants and is open to the public. According to _____, "Several recent studies have concluded that the ability to get along well with people at work has become more important than technical competence. People are working in teams now more than ever before and need to be able to develop their emotional intelligence in order to be successful. This workshop helps people begin the process of developing those competencies."

_____ is a licensed _____ in private practice in _____. S/he specializes in _____ and _____. For reservations, call _____ at (_____) _____-_____.

Exhibit 4.1 Presentation Outline

Increasing Emotional Intelligence in the Workplace

Topic	Time Estimate
I. Introduction	
A. Introduce yourself	1 minute
B. Ask group members to introduce themselves	10 minutes
C. State workshop goals	1 minute
II. The importance of people skills	1 minute
III. What Emotional Intelligence is	5 minutes
IV. What Emotional Intelligence is not	5 minutes
V. 25 competencies	18 minutes
VI. Emotional Intelligence quiz	15 minutes
VII. Four key competencies	
A. Emotional awareness	1 minute
Video exercise 1	7 minutes
Video exercise 2	6 minutes
B. Accurate self-assessment	
Video exercise	5 minutes
C. Understanding others	
Video exercise	6 minutes
D. Communication	16–26 minutes
Video exercise	3 minutes
VIII. Conclude workshop	3 minutes
Approximate total time	**103–113 minutes**

Exhibit 4.2   Presentation Script

Increasing Emotional Intelligence in the Workplace

Outline	Presenter's Comments	Activity
I-A. **Introduce Yourself**	My name is _____. I'm a licensed _____, with a _____. I specialize in working with _____, and became interested in the importance of "people skills" in the workplace when _____.	Refer to your bio on the first page of the handouts. 1 minute.
I-B. **Group Intro** ⏱	I'd like to begin today's workshop by finding out a bit about each of you. Let's go around the room and each of you give your name and tell us something about yourself.	If the group is under 20 people, ask participants to introduce themselves. 10 minutes.
I-C. **Goals**	Based on Daniel Goleman's book *Emotional Intelligence at Work,* this workshop will help you: • Recognize how emotions affect work behavior and performance. • Assess your emotional strengths and limitations. • Assess work experiences and identify areas where you wish to do things differently. • Respond to challenging work situations with appropriate empathy and listening skills. • Negotiate and resolve disagreements.	State goals. 1 minute.
II. **The Importance of People Skills**	It is an understatement that the world of work is changing. In most companies, there are fewer people doing more work. This means that people skills are more critical than ever. Technical competence is important, but skills like working as part of a team, leading others, and managing emotions have become even more meaningful. In *Emotional Intelligence at Work,* author Daniel Goleman summarizes research from almost 500 corporations, government agencies, and nonprofit organizations. He says that dozens of researchers independently arrived at the "remarkably similar conclusions" outlined in this book: that in virtually any job today, the 25 competencies that make up what he calls Emotional Intelligence are far more important than technical competence or intellectual brilliance.	Present information. 1 minute.

Outline	Presenter's Comments	Activity
III. **What** **Emotional** **Intelligence Is**	Emotional Intelligence (EI) is the ability to quickly recognize emotional responses to situations and people, and to use that knowledge in effective ways. Having emotional intelligence means being able to do the following (participants may want to note these on Handout 4.1):	Handout 4.1. Present information. Participants may take notes. 5 minutes.

- Know what you're feeling and use that knowledge to make good decisions.
- Manage distressing feelings; calm yourself when you feel anxious and manage anger appropriately.
- Maintain hope in the face of setbacks.
- Have empathy for others.
- Get along with most people.

Outline	Presenter's Comments	Activity
IV. **What EI Is** **Not**	Emotional Intelligence is *not* any of the following:	Handout 4.1. Present information. Participants may take notes. 5 minutes.

1. Being nice.
2. Letting it all hang out.
3. Something you are either born with or without. EI can be increased in adulthood, but, like other abilities, it must be carefully developed.
4. A list of ways in which women are smarter than men.
5. A list of ways in which men are smarter than women. Both genders have strengths and weaknesses. Studies show that most women are taught to be more aware of people's feelings, so in general they are more skilled at empathy. But men are often better at dismissing upsetting feelings. They may distract themselves by watching a game on television, while women tend to ponder what's bothering them.

There are many ways to develop your emotional intelligence. You can learn emotional skills at any point, and the odds that you'll have a happy, successful life are much greater if you do.

Goleman outlines 25 distinct competencies in *Working with Emotional Intelligence.* Since our time is limited, we will first present an overview of what Goleman's work means to you, followed by a brief exploration of four of the competencies.

As you participate in today's workshop, think about how your company *encourages* these competencies or *discourages* them. The more your company encourages them, the more productive and effective it will be.

Outline	Presenter's Comments	Activity
V. **25 Competencies**	You will find a list of Goleman's 25 competencies on Handout 4.2. Rather than just read through them (which you can do after the workshop), let's see what they mean on the job.	Handout 4.2. Individual exercise. 10 minutes.
	On the second page of the handout, you will find three vignettes describing some common workplace scenarios. Each vignette illustrates several of the competencies (or their absence).	
	Read each of the three vignettes and, for each, identify which competencies (or their absence) are illustrated. Give yourself about 10 minutes to complete the handout. When you are finished, we'll discuss each vignette and see what you came up with.	
	Answers to look for: Vignette #1 demonstrates the *absence* of the following: emotional awareness, self-control, understanding of others, developing of others, communication, leadership, building of bonds, collaboration and cooperation, and team capabilities. Vignette #2 demonstrates self-confidence, innovation, achievement drive, commitment, initiative, optimism, and leadership. She appears to *lack* accurate self-assessment, understanding of others, developing of others, political awareness, influence, communication, collaboration and cooperation, and team capabilities. Vignette #3 demonstrates self-confidence and achievement drive. He appears to lack understanding of others, developing of others, leveraging of diversity, political awareness, communication, leadership, change catalyst, building of bonds, collaboration and cooperation, and team capabilities.	Group discussion of vignettes and answers. 10 minutes.
VI. **EI Quiz**	Handout 4.3 is an EI Quiz. Test yourself on how well you understand the competencies of EI. You may refer to the list on Handout 4.2.	Handout 4.3 Complete quiz. 5 minutes.
	Take about five minutes to complete the quiz.	
	Now let's discuss the answers together.	Discuss quiz. 10 minutes.
	1. I am always aware of my feelings in the present moment. *Emotional awareness* 2. I sense what people are feeling without them telling me. *Understanding others*	

3. I have a difficult time handling conflict and disagreements in my relationships. *Conflict management*

4. I have compassion for others' situations because I have such a strong sense of what they are feeling. *Understanding others*

5. I usually explode when I'm angry. *Self-control*

6. When I feel upset, I can put a lid on my feelings and stay focused on what I need to accomplish. *Self-control*

7. If I feel nervous about a presentation or exam, I tend to become overwhelmed and it's hard for me to prepare. *Self-control*

8. I can sense what other people are feeling, even though nothing has been stated. *Understanding others*

9. I am very impulsive and easily distracted from my goals. *Self-control*

10. I rely on my feelings to make important decisions in my life. *Emotional awareness*

11. When I feel angry, I keep my feelings to myself. *Self-control*

12. I stay hopeful and optimistic when I experience setbacks or disappointments. I never give up. *Optimism*

13. I am always trying to do better. *Achievement drive*

14. I sometimes feel overwhelmed by my emotions. *Self-control*

15. I don't get upset when I'm asked to change the way I do something. *Adaptability*

VII. Four Key Competencies

Goleman explains why these skills are so important today. He writes, "In today's workplace, at all job levels, these are the skills that people need to succeed. As work becomes more complex and collaborative, companies where people work together best have a competitive edge" (page 29).

Let's take a look at four of the competencies:

1. Emotional awareness
2. Accurate self-assessment
3. Understanding others
4. Communication

Present information.

1 minute.

Outline	Presenter's Comments	Activity
VII-A. **Emotional** **Awareness**	The first competency we're going to explore is emotional awareness: recognizing your emotions and their effects. We will illustrate it with a video example—one that shows a person who lacks emotional awareness.	
🕐 **Video Exercise**	In the movie *The Remains of the Day,* butler Mr. Stevens (Anthony Hopkins) shows little emotion. When his father dies during a large dinner at the estate, he carries on with his work and demonstrates a complete absence of emotion.	Show video. 2 minutes.
	According to Goleman, people who are emotionally aware:	Present information.
	• Are able to recognize their own emotions and the effects of those emotions. Do you think Mr. Stevens recognized his own emotions? (It doesn't seem so.)	Ask discussion questions. 5 minutes.
	• Know *what* they are feeling and understand *why* they are feeling it.	
	• Understand how their feelings are related to their thoughts, actions, and the things they say.	
	• Recognize how their feelings affect their performance.	
	A person who *excels* in this area is aware of his or her emotions. It means tuning in to yourself and even being aware of how your emotions feel physically.	
🕐 **Video Exercise**	In the movie *Good Will Hunting,* Sean Maguire (Robin Williams) demonstrates empathy. *(Show the scene where Sean Maguire tells Will Hunting [Matt Damon], "It's not your fault." Will cries and embraces Sean. This scene is toward the end of the movie.)*	Show video. 2 minutes.
	(Note: An alternative is to show the scene at the end of Titanic *where Jack [Leonardo DiCaprio] dies. You may have another idea for a scene; anything that demonstrates strong emotion will do.)*	
	How did the scene make you feel? How did you feel physically as you watched it?	Lead discussion. 2 minutes.
	This awareness is what we are talking about. It requires slowing down and paying attention to what is going on inside of you. It requires some discipline—sometimes you have to force yourself to shut out the world and allow yourself to be introspective.	Summarize. 1 minute.
	Why do you think self-awareness is an important quality, especially in a work context?	Lead discussion. 1 minute.

4.10

Outline	Presenter's Comments	Activity

Answer to look for:

People who are cut off from their emotions are unable to connect with people. No one wants to work with such people because they lack awareness of how they affect others.

VII-B.
Accurate Self-Assessment

The second competency is *accurate self-assessment*. It means knowing your strengths and limits. Let's look at an example of a movie character who seems to completely lack this ability—but starts to develop it, with a little help from his fellow characters.

Present information.

Video Exercise

In the movie *As Good As It Gets,* Melvin Udall (Jack Nicholson) seems to have no awareness of how his behavior impacts others. *(There are many scenes to choose from; two suggestions are the opening scene in the hallway [with the dog] and the first scene in the restaurant, where Nicholson insults almost everyone present. Be aware of strong language that may offend some participants.)*

Show video.
2 minutes.

What are some other examples of people who lack this competency, as well as those who possess it?

Lead discussion.
3 minutes.

Note your own examples here:

VII-C.
Understanding Others

The third competency is *understanding others*. This means sensing others' feelings and perspectives and taking an active interest in their concerns.

Video Exercise

Again in the movie *The Remains of the Day,* Anthony Hopkins's character, Mr. Stevens, seems to have no emotions. Early in the movie, when Mr. Stevens tells his father that he is no longer allowed to work, he pays no attention to his father's protests.

Show video.
2 minutes.

How do you think Mr. Stevens's father felt?

What are some other examples of people who possess this ability?

Lead discussion.
4 minutes.

Outline	Presenter's Comments	Activity

VII-D.
Communication

Do you remember hearing about the Peter Principle? Who can state what it says?

Lead discussion.

1 minute.

Answer:

The Peter Principle states that people get promoted until they reach their level of incompetence.

Most of us in today's companies work in groups. In terms of the Peter Principle, today's workers still rise to the level of their incompetence. However, incompetence now manifests itself most often as a lack of emotional intelligence.

Present information.

2 minutes.

For example, Dave is a star technician who has been promoted several times. If Dave is to advance any further, he must solicit help from others. Now he must learn how to listen, persuade, be patient, contain his emotions, offer sympathy, feel empathy, and recover from the emotional onslaughts that come with group give-and-take. One of the most important competencies for people like Dave is the fourth on our list—communication.

Video Exercise

In the movie *Wall Street,* Gordon Gecko (Michael Douglas) is ruthless, greedy, and arrogant. He shows no interest in the opinions or requests of anyone. (*Show the scene early in the movie where Bud Fox [Charlie Sheen] nervously meets Gordon Gecko for the first time.*)

Show video.

2 minutes.

What grade would you give Gordon Gecko for listening? What did he say or do that leads you to this conclusion?

Lead discussion.

1 minute.

In *Working with Emotional Intelligence,* Goleman says that people with the competence of listening openly and sending convincing messages demonstrate the following four behaviors (participants may wish to list them on Handout 4.4):

Handout 4.4.

Present information.

3 minutes.

1. They are effective in give-and-take, registering emotional cues in attuning their message.

2. They deal with difficult issues straightforwardly.

3. They listen well, seek mutual understanding, and welcome sharing of information fully.

4. They foster open communication and stay receptive to bad news as well as good.

(*Working with Emotional Intelligence,* page 174)

4.12

Outline	Presenter's Comments	Activity

Handout 4.5 will give us some practice with some examples. Let's look at each item and talk about what makes it effective or not.

Handout 4.5.

1. Pay attention to the speaker's nonverbal behavior and think about its meaning. This is important because the other person's nonverbal behavior gives you clues about what they are thinking and feeling. When you acknowledge another person's way of presenting him- or herself, it makes them feel good. For example, what if Mr. Stevens had commented on his father's obvious distress when he told him he could no longer work? His father would have felt better about what he was being asked to do.

Present information.

Ask for examples and encourage discussion as time allows.

10–20 minutes.

2. Ask what a word means when you don't understand it. Asking for clarification means that you are interested. It is also an acknowledgment that you are not all-knowing and gives the other person permission to be less than perfect, too.

3. Think about your answer before the speaker has finished talking. Most of us do this occasionally, but it is distracting when it becomes obvious that the listener has stopped listening. It also conveys the message that the speaker is less important.

4. Look at the speaker while he or she is talking. This is very important in American culture. It demonstrates respect and interest. In other cultures, it has other meanings.

5. Pay attention to your own emotional responses as the speaker is talking. Being aware of what you are feeling as you listen to another gives you a greater ability to respond more fully and accurately.

6. Think about the best way to convey your message: speaking, writing, telephone, and so on. If you want to convey your thoughts and opinions accurately and completely, some ways are better than others. It depends on the situation. Example: Barbara has a boss who communicates with her only through e-mail. She says it feels very awkward most of the time. How effective is that?

7. Tune in to the other person and think about how he or she may be feeling. When Bud Fox visited Gordon Gecko for the first time, he was thoroughly intimidated. Gecko seemed to enjoy it. Rather than using this awareness to help Fox calm down, Gecko seemed to

4.13

enjoy making him even more anxious. When people are highly anxious, they have much less access to their abilities and knowledge.

8. When you don't agree with the speaker, you tune him or her out. You know when you are on the receiving end of this, and it never feels good. It only makes communication less effective.

9. Pay attention to what is being said, even if you aren't really interested. If it is genuine, it makes interactions more pleasant. It is okay to assertively say that you are not interested, too.

10. When you think that you already know what the speaker is going to say, stop paying attention. This is ineffective because you may be wrong; perhaps the speaker will surprise you. It demonstrates a lack of respect for the speaker to assume that you can read his or her mind. When you are on the receiving end of this situation, it never feels good.

11. Summarize in your own words what you heard the speaker say. This is effective and promotes understanding.

12. Listen to what the speaker is saying, even if you have a different view. Keeping an open mind demonstrates that you are flexible and looking for new viewpoints. Welcoming diverse opinions will enhance your ability to create something completely new.

**VIII.
Conclude
Workshop**

In our short time together, we have covered a lot of ground. Let's spend a moment looking at how you can further develop your EI abilities.

Present information.

3 minutes.

You can learn emotional skills at any point, and the odds that you'll have a happy, successful life are much greater if you do. Here are some suggestions:

- Encourage your company to offer training programs that focus on the skills we've explored today.
- Work on developing the skills with the help of a licensed psychotherapist.
- Look for a support group or group therapy.
- Being in a good marriage helps develop these skills.

It's never too late to get smart about feelings, and the effort is worth it.

I hope you have enjoyed today's workshop. In the time remaining, I would be happy to answer any questions you may have.

Handout 4.1 What Is Emotional Intelligence?

Emotional Intelligence *is:*

1. _____

2. _____

3. _____

4. _____

5. _____

Emotional Intelligence is *not:*

1. _____

2. _____

3. _____

4. _____

5. _____

Handout 4.2   The Emotional Competence Framework

Personal Competence

These competencies determine how we manage ourselves.

Self-awareness
Knowing one's internal states, preferences, resources, and intuitions

- **Emotional awareness:** Recognizing one's emotions and their effects
- **Accurate self-assessment:** Knowing one's strengths and limits
- **Self-confidence:** A strong sense of one's self-worth and capabilities

Self-regulation
Managing one's internal states, impulses, and resources

- **Self-control:** Keeping disruptive emotions and impulses in check
- **Trustworthiness:** Maintaining standards of honesty and integrity
- **Conscientiousness:** Taking responsibility for personal performance
- **Adaptability:** Flexibility in handling change
- **Innovation:** Being comfortable with novel ideas, approaches, and new information

Motivation
Emotional tendencies that guide or facilitate reaching goals

- **Achievement drive:** Striving to improve or meet a standard of excellence
- **Commitment:** Aligning with the goals of the group or organization
- **Initiative:** Readiness to act on opportunities
- **Optimism:** Persistence in pursuing goals despite obstacles and setbacks

Social Competence

These competencies determine how we handle relationships.

Empathy
Awareness of others' feelings, needs, and concerns

- **Understanding others:** Sensing others' feelings and perspectives, and taking an active interest in their concerns
- **Developing others:** Sensing others' development needs and bolstering their abilities
- **Service orientation:** Anticipating, recognizing, and meeting customers' needs
- **Leveraging diversity:** Cultivating opportunities through different kinds of people
- **Political awareness:** Reading a group's emotional currents and power relationships

Social skills
Adeptness at inducing desirable responses in others

- **Influence:** Wielding effective tactics for persuasion
- **Communication:** Listening openly and sending convincing messages
- **Conflict management:** Negotiating and resolving disagreements
- **Leadership:** Inspiring and guiding individuals and groups
- **Change catalyst:** Initiating or managing change
- **Building bonds:** Nurturing instrumental relationships
- **Collaboration and cooperation:** Working with others toward shared goals
- **Team capabilities:** Creating group synergy in pursuing collective goals

Source: From *Working with Emotional Intelligence* by Daniel Goleman. Copyright © 1998 by Daniel Goleman. Used by permission of Bantam Books, a division of Random House, Inc.

1. Lisa is an instructional designer in a consulting firm. She has many years of experience and does excellent work. The owner of the firm, Jared Rosenblatt, is very unfriendly and intimidating. He has never called Lisa by name or spent any time with her one on one in the 10 months she has been on his staff. Even though it is a very small company, he never looks up when he passes her in the hallway and says nothing when he passes her desk during the day. He often has temper tantrums and screams at people when he is under pressure. Last week, Lisa was the target of his rage. Every day she feels a knot in her stomach on the way to work.

   Which competencies does Jared demonstrate? _____

   _____

   _____

   _____

   _____

   Which competencies does he appear to lack? _____

   _____

   _____

   _____

   _____

2. Sarah Jackson is the manager of a large department. She is a very flamboyant woman who was brought in from outside the company two years ago. She produces good results and her bosses are, for the most, part happy with her performance. She is quite creative and her staff has introduced several new products in the past few months. She has become famous for her pep rallies and contests. Everyone in her area knows that she expects total commitment to the company and they all work hard. Recently, however, four of her key people resigned to form their own company. They said they were tired of Sarah's iron fist and excessive work demands.

   Which competencies does Sarah demonstrate? _____

   _____

   _____

   _____

   Which competencies does she appear to lack? _____

   _____

   _____

   _____

   _____

3. Bill MacIntyre became the vice president of human resources six months ago. He was brought in from a sister division in another state. He is a handsome man and fits right in with the look of the executive committee. He makes a very charming first impression. In the time he's been here, though, Bill's staff members have all begun to look for jobs outside the company. They say that he is gradually replacing them with his own people. They think he plans to build his own empire and doesn't want any of the old staffers to be a part of it. He has had only one staff meeting, and that was in his first week on the job.

Which competencies does Bill demonstrate? _____

_____

_____

_____

_____

Which competencies does he appear to lack? _____

_____

_____

_____

_____

Handout 4.3   Emotional Intelligence Quiz

Description of Behavior or Attitude   **Competence**

1. I am always aware of my feelings in the present moment.   _____

2. I sense what people are feeling without them telling me.   _____

3. I have a difficult time handling conflict and disagreements in my
   relationships.   _____

4. I have compassion for others' situations because I have such a strong
   sense of what they are feeling.   _____

5. I usually explode when I'm angry.   _____

6. When I feel upset, I can put a lid on my feelings and stay focused on
   what I need to accomplish.   _____

7. If I feel nervous about a presentation or exam, I tend to become
   overwhelmed and it's hard for me to prepare.   _____

8. I can sense what other people are feeling, even though nothing has
   been stated.   _____

9. I am very impulsive and easily distracted from my goals.   _____

10. I rely on my feelings to make important decisions in my life.   _____

11. When I feel angry, I keep my feelings to myself.   _____

12. I stay hopeful and optimistic when I experience setbacks or
    disappointments. I never give up.   _____

13. I am always trying to do better.   _____

14. I sometimes feel overwhelmed by my emotions.   _____

15. I don't get upset when I'm asked to change the way I do something. _____

Handout 4.4 Communication Skills

Listening openly and sending convincing messages include the following four skills:

1. _____

2. _____

3. _____

4. _____

Handout 4.5   Listening Behavior

Indicate which of the following listening behaviors encourage clarity and serve to maintain the self-esteem of the speaker.

_____ 1.   Pay attention to the speaker's nonverbal behavior and think about its meaning.

_____ 2.   Ask what a word means when you don't understand it.

_____ 3.   Think about your answer before the speaker has finished talking.

_____ 4.   Look at the speaker while he or she is talking.

_____ 5.   Pay attention to your own emotional responses as the speaker is talking.

_____ 6.   Think about the best way to convey your message: speaking, writing, telephone, and so on.

_____ 7.   Tune in to the other person and think about how he or she may be feeling.

_____ 8.   When you don't agree with the speaker, tune him or her out.

_____ 9.   Pay attention to what is being said, even if you aren't really interested.

_____ 10.   When you think you know what the speaker is going to say, stop paying attention.

_____ 11.   Summarize in your own words what you heard the speaker say.

_____ 12.   Listen to what the speaker is saying, even if you have a different view.

Chapter 5

How to Give Constructive Performance Feedback

Presentation Synopsis

Managing people requires knowing how to give employees constructive, specific feedback about their job performance. Unfortunately, many employees never know whether they are doing their jobs properly because feedback is communicated ineffectively. In this workshop, participants will learn five basic steps of giving an employee specific performance feedback. Skills will be developed through lecture, demonstration, and a variety of practice exercises.

Time Requirements

This presentation runs from 1 hour to 1½ hours, depending on the style of the presenter and the number of interactive activities used.

⏱ **Clock symbol.** This means that the information is included for a longer seminar or workshop. Omit these sections for a shorter presentation. If time is limited, another way to shorten your presentation is to share the information in lecture format. However, keep in mind that it is often harder to engage and maintain the audience's interest with pure lecture style. Unless you are a particularly dynamic speaker, you will probably want to keep at least a few of the exercises to enliven the presentation.

Video examples. Showing selected scenes from popular movies is one way to make your presentation more interesting. It creates some variety and interest, stimulates discussion, and might be a way to inject some humor. Consider selecting short scenes from videos such as *Jerry Maguire*. Suggestions for specific scenes are included in this outline, but you are encouraged to look for other examples on your own as you prepare for your presentation.

How to Use This Presentation

Possible Audiences	Whom to Contact
Adult education groups at churches and synagogues	Director of adult education programs
PTO/PTA	PTO/PTA president
Women's civic and professional organizations	Director of educational programs

Sample Text for Marketing Letter, Brochure, or Postcard

Managing people requires knowing how to give employees constructive, specific feedback about their job performance. Unfortunately, many employees never know whether they are doing their jobs properly because feedback is communicated ineffectively. In this workshop, participants will learn five basic steps of giving an employee specific performance feedback. Skills will be developed through lecture, demonstration, and a variety of practice exercises.

_____ is a licensed _____ in private practice in _____. S/he specializes in _____ and _____. Call _____ today to schedule your group's **free** workshop. (_____) _____-_____.

Sample Text for Press Release

_____ Presents Personal Growth Workshop

_____ is presenting a **free** workshop on how to give constructive performance feedback to employees in the workplace. The workshop is scheduled for _____, from _____ to _____ at _____. The workshop is limited to ____ participants and is open to the public.

According to _____, "Managing people requires knowing how to give employees constructive, specific feedback about their job performance. Unfortunately, many employees never know whether they are doing their jobs properly because feedback is communicated ineffectively." In this workshop, participants will learn five basic steps of giving an employee specific performance feedback. Skills will be developed through lecture, demonstration, and a variety of practice exercises.

_____ is a licensed _____ in private practice in _____. S/he specializes in _____ and _____. For reservations, call _____at (_____) _____-_____.

Exhibit 5.1   Presentation Outline

How to Give Constructive Performance Feedback

Topic	Time Estimate
I. Introduction	
A. Introduce yourself	1 minute
B. Ask group members to introduce themselves	10 minutes
C. State workshop goals	1 minute
II. Why feedback is important	5 minutes
Video example	
III. Analysis of cases	15 minutes
IV. Steps for giving feedback	5 minutes
V. Principles for giving feedback	15 minutes
VI. Practice exercises	14 minutes
VII. Role-play	15 minutes
VIII. Conclusion	
Approximate total time	**81 minutes**

Exhibit 5.2 Presentation Script

How to Give Constructive Performance Feedback

Outline	Presenter's Comments	Activity
I-A. **Introduce Yourself**	My name is _____. I'm a licensed _____, with a _____. I specialize in working with _____, and became interested in the kinds of problems people encounter at work about _____ ago, when _____ _____.	Refer to your bio on the first page of the handouts. 1 minute.
I-B. **Group Intro** ⏱	I'd like to begin today's workshop by finding out a bit about each of you. Let's go around the room and each person tell us your name and where you work.	If the group is under 20 people, ask participants to introduce themselves. 10 minutes.
I-C. **Goals**	In this workshop, you will learn five basic steps of giving an employee specific performance feedback.	State goals. 1 minute.
II. **Why Feedback Is Important**	Let's begin our discussion by taking a look at some typical examples of what goes on in work environments when managers *don't* give good feedback.	Introduce subject.
⏱ **Video Example**	As an example of what can happen when effective performance feedback is not given, I'd like to show you a scene from a recent movie. Early in the movie *Jerry Maguire,* Jerry (played by Tom Cruise) is fired from his job. What was wrong with the way Jerry's boss handled this situation?	Show video. Lead discussion. 5 minutes.

Possible answers:

- He gave no warning.
- There was no chance to improve.
- The reasons were unclear.
- It was carried out in a public place.
- It was unnecessarily humiliating.

What are some other examples of what can happen when performance feedback is given poorly or not at all?

Outline	Presenter's Comments	Activity
III. **Analysis of** **Cases**	Please take about three minutes to complete Handout 5.1.	Handout 5.1. Individual exercise. Group discussion. 10 minutes.

Let's take a few minutes to discuss each item on the handout. Note that there are no right answers to these questions; they are for stimulating thought and discussion.

1. John has been working at his new job for one month. On his first day at work, Wilma, his boss, showed him what to do and got him started on a project. Since then, Wilma has communicated with him mostly through voice mail and e-mail. She walks past his cubicle and says hello a few times each day, but there hasn't been much other communication. John is assuming he is doing his job properly, but he really isn't sure.

Look for answers like these:

- What is wrong with the feedback to this employee?

  There is no feedback here. John has no idea whether he is doing his job properly.

- What should the manager do instead?

  Wilma should have given John a detailed job description on the first day. She should have gone over his first project as soon as he completed it, making certain he understood the task and completed it properly. She also should have checked in with him regularly to make certain he is doing his job correctly and to see whether he has any questions.

2. Stella works in an office. Yesterday, she spent several hours filing a huge stack of folders that her boss had given her in the morning. When she got to work today, her boss came over to her desk and yelled, "Stella! You did those files all wrong! Don't you *listen?*" He said it so loudly that Stella's three office mates turned toward her in shock. He went back into his office and slammed the door.

Look for answers like these:

- What is wrong with the feedback to this employee?

  This manager's behavior is abusive. It lowers Stella's self-esteem and frightens her coworkers. An atmosphere of fear also lowers productivity and encourages sabotage and turnover.

- What should the manager do instead?

  He should have delivered the feedback calmly and in private. He should also have asked her for her understanding of the task; perhaps there was a reason for it being done the way it was. Third, he should be specific about what she did wrong.

3. Angela asked Steve, her assistant, to call a list of 20 clients and set up phone interviews for *next* Thursday and Friday (the 20th and 21st). She provided Steve with an updated list of phone numbers and told him the hours she would be available to speak with the clients. When Angela came back from lunch today, Steve had left a list of interviews on her desk. He had set them up for *this* Thursday and Friday (the 13th and 14th). He also had written next to four of the clients' names, "wrong phone number." As she picks up the phone to reschedule the first client, she says to herself, "See, you just can't get good help these days."

Look for answers like these:

- What is wrong with the feedback to this employee?

  As far as we can tell, there was no feedback to this employee.

- What should the manager do instead?

  Employees don't learn if they are not given feedback. This manager should have talked to Steve calmly and in private. She should also ask Steve what he understood the task to be and why he scheduled the interviews for the wrong dates. Finally, she should ask Steve to reschedule the calls for the correct dates.

What are some of your own examples of times when performance feedback was not given effectively? What could have been done differently to make the situation better?

Group discussion.

5 minutes.

IV.
Steps for
Giving
Feedback

Now that we've looked at a few examples of what can happen when performance feedback *isn't* given effectively, let's talk about some principles for doing it well. We'll use the third vignette on Handout 5.1 to illustrate how this might look.

Present information.

Outline	Presenter's Comments	Activity
	Suggest that participants write the five steps on Handout 5.2. They are:	Handout 5.2. List the five steps. Use the third vignette from Handout 5.1 to illustrate each step. 5 minutes.

Suggest that participants write the five steps on Handout 5.2. They are:

1. *Describe the situation.*

   "Steve, these appointments are all scheduled for the 13th and 14th. I asked you to schedule them for the 20th and 21st."

2. *Ask the employee for his or her view of the situation.*

   "Tell me, what was your understanding of what I asked you to do?"

3. *Come to an understanding of the situation.*

   "So you just misunderstood what I wanted. I had written the dates in my note to you, but you didn't read it thoroughly before you started making the calls."

4. *Develop an action plan to take to resolve the situation.*

   "I would like you to reschedule all of these appointments before 5:00 today. What will it take for you to do that?"

5. *Agree to follow up later to make certain the situation has been resolved.*

   "I'll check in with you at 4:30 to see how you are doing with this." At 4:30, stop by Steve's desk and ask, "How are you doing on your calls?"

V. Principles for Giving Feedback

Life is a bit more complicated than these five simple steps. Let's look at Handout 5.3 for some other issues to consider.

Please take about five minutes to complete the eight true-false questions on the handout. Then we will go over them together.

1. Giving feedback is most effective when it is written down.

   True. Having it in writing increases the chances that it will be understood. For example, Angela could simply note the dates and times she is available and hand it to Steve. She could also write "by 5 P.M. today" at the top.

2. You don't need to worry about the employee becoming upset. As the boss, you have the right to tell people what to do and not worry about their feelings.

   False. Being concerned about other people's feelings is important in any situation. Effective managers demonstrate concern for the self-esteem of their team members. This doesn't mean withholding criticism or ignoring problems.

Activity (for section V): Handout 5.3.

Individual exercise.

5 minutes.

Ask participants for their answers before you give yours.

Lead group discussion of answers to items on Handout 5.3.

10 minutes.

3. Only newer employees need this kind of feedback.

   False. All employees need feedback.

4. Feedback should be as specific as possible.

   True. People have a difficult time responding to instructions that are vague and unclear. It is important to check for understanding; avoid assuming that you are on the same wavelength.

5. It's not necessary to take the time to think through what you want to say before giving feedback.

   False. Taking the time to gather your thoughts and clarify what you want your feedback to accomplish increases the chances that you will communicate clearly.

6. Get the employee's point of view *before* you state what you think should be done.

   True. People are more receptive when they have a chance to explain themselves first. You might also learn something unexpected that will explain the situation or change your point of view.

7. It is okay to withhold feedback when employees are new. You don't want to criticize too much and cause them to feel discouraged.

   False. People need to know how they are doing.

8. If you see that the employee corrected a problem situation, then you don't need to follow up.

   False. When you follow up, you are telling employees that you are being thorough and that the work is important.

VI. Practice Exercises

Please take about seven minutes to complete the exercise on Handout 5.4 individually.

Situation #1: As you check the copies you asked your assistant to make for tomorrow's presentation, you see that he made one-sided copies, three-hole-punched. You had asked for two-sided copies, without holes. This is the second time he has made this type of mistake in the past week.

1. *Describe the situation.*

   "Jim, these copies aren't right. I asked you to make two-sided copies without holes. You made one-sided copies with holes."

Handout 5.4.

Individual exercise.

7 minutes.

Discuss answers together.

7 minutes.

2. *Ask the employee for his or her view of the situation.*

"What can you tell me about how this happened?"

3. Come to an understanding of the situation.

"How can you prevent this from happening again?"

4. Develop an action plan to take to resolve the situation.

"Please redo these as soon as you can. I need them by noon."

5. Agree to follow up later to make certain the situation has been resolved.

"Jim, thanks for having these copies redone even earlier than I'd asked for them."

Situation #2: You arrive at work planning to interview five candidates for an open position in your department. Your assistant has scheduled the interviews. She will be in late today because of a prearranged doctor's appointment. Five minutes before the first applicant arrives, you open the file marked "Employment Applications," and you see that it is empty. After 15 minutes of searching, you find the applications in your assistant's drawer. You begin the first interview 10 minutes late.

1. *Describe the situation.*

"Sue, I couldn't find the employment applications for my interviews when I got here this morning. I had to search your desk for them and started my first interview 10 minutes late."

2. *Ask the employee for his or her view of the situation.*

"What can you tell me about how this happened?"

3. *Come to an understanding of the situation.*

"How can you prevent this from happening again?"

4. *Develop an action plan to take to resolve the situation.*

"Please be sure to give me the applications for my next set of candidates before you leave next time."

5. *Agree to follow up later to make certain the situation has been resolved.*

(The next time there are interviews scheduled) "Sue, please be sure to give me the folder of applications for tomorrow's candidates before you leave tonight. Okay?"

Outline	Presenter's Comments	Activity

Situation #3: A fax arrives at 4:30 P.M. from a client requesting some important information needed by 9:00 the next morning. You must leave for a meeting outside the office right then, and you ask your assistant to complete the assignment before leaving for the day. You explain the urgency of the task and she agrees to stay until it is done. When you arrive the next morning at 8:30 A.M., you find a note from your assistant that says, "Sorry, I couldn't find the information you wanted." You hurriedly find the needed information and fax it to the client. Your assistant arrives at her desk at her scheduled starting time of 9:00 A.M.

1. *Describe the situation.*

   "Pauline, when I came in this morning, I had to scramble to find that information for the client."

2. *Ask the employee for his or her view of the situation.*

   "What can you tell me about how this happened?"

3. *Come to an understanding of the situation.*

   "How can you prevent this from happening again?"

4. *Develop an action plan to take to resolve the situation.*

   "If you ever have a similar problem and I'm not here, please ask Marianne to help you. If you still can't find it, please leave me a voice mail letting me know what happened. If I'd known you couldn't find it, I would have come in earlier today. You could have come in early, too."

5. *Agree to follow up later to make certain the situation has been resolved.*

   (The current situation was resolved, but let's say that a similar one happened later.) "If you have any problem with this, you'll call me, right?"

VII.
Role-play

Let's read the three vignettes on Handout 5.5. I'd like two volunteers to role-play these vignettes. One person will play the role of the supervisor, and the other is the employee.

Ask the person in the role of the supervisor to give constructive feedback to the employee, following the five steps.

Ask the rest of the participants to take notes on what the person in the role of the supervisor says or does to demonstrate each point.

Handout 5.5.

Follow instructions on handout for role-play.

Conduct role-play.

Participants take notes as role-play proceeds.

10 minutes.

Outline	Presenter's Comments	Activity
	Which steps were demonstrated most clearly?	Lead group discussion.
	Keep the feedback discussion as positive as possible. When an observer has a critical comment, ask the group to think of what the supervisor could have said or done instead.	5 minutes.
VIII. Conclusion	I hope you have enjoyed today's workshop. In the time remaining, I would be happy to answer any questions you may have.	Conclude the workshop.

Handout 5.1 What Is Constructive Performance Feedback?

1. John has been working at his new job for one month. On his first day at work, Wilma, his boss, showed him what to do and got him started on a project. Since then, Wilma has communicated with him mostly through voice mail and e-mail. She walks past his cubicle and says hello a few times each day, but there hasn't been much other communication. John is assuming he is doing his job properly, but he really isn't sure.

   • What is wrong with the feedback to this employee?

   _____

   • What should the manager do instead?

   _____

2. Stella works in an office. Yesterday, she spent several hours filing a huge stack of folders that her boss had given her in the morning. When she got to work today, her boss came over to her desk and yelled, "Stella! You did those files all wrong! Don't you *listen?*" He said it so loudly that Stella's three office mates turned toward her in shock. He went back into his office and slammed the door.

   • What is wrong with the feedback to this employee?

   _____

   • What should the manager do instead?

   _____

3. Angela asked Steve, her assistant, to call a list of 20 clients and set up phone interviews for *next* Thursday and Friday (the 20th and 21st). She provided Steve with an updated list of phone numbers and told him the hours she would be available to speak with the clients. When Angela came back from lunch today, Steve had left a list of interviews on her desk. He had set them up for *this* Thursday and Friday (the 13th and 14th). He also had written next to four of the clients' names, "wrong phone number." As she picks up the phone to reschedule the first client, she says to herself, "See, you just can't get good help these days."

   • What is wrong with the feedback to this employee?

   _____

   • What should the manager do instead?

   _____

Handout 5.2   Giving Constructive Performance Feedback

Action steps:

1. _____

2. _____

3. _____

4. _____

5. _____

Handout 5.3   Other Considerations

True or False? Circle one.

T or F   1. Giving feedback is most effective when it is written down.

T   F   2. You don't need to worry about the employee becoming upset. As the boss, you have the right to tell people what to do and not worry about their feelings.

T   F   3. Only newer employees need this kind of feedback.

T   F   4. Feedback should be as specific as possible.

T   F   5. It's not necessary to take the time to think through what you want to say before giving feedback.

T   F   6. Get the employee's point of view *before* you state what you think should be done.

T   F   7. It is okay to withhold feedback when employees are new. You don't want to criticize too much and cause them to feel discouraged.

T   F   8. If you see that the employee corrected a problem situation, then you don't need to follow up.

Handout 5.4   Practice Exercises

For each of the following three situations, write what you would say for each of the five steps. Use the worksheets on the following pages to write your script for each situation.

1. As you check the copies you asked your assistant to make for tomorrow's presentation, you see that he made one-sided copies, three-hole-punched. You had asked for two-sided copies, without holes. This is the second time he has made this type of mistake in the past week.

2. You arrive at work planning to interview five candidates for an open position in your department. Your assistant has scheduled the interviews. She will be in late today because of a pre-arranged doctor's appointment. Five minutes before the first applicant arrives, you open the file marked "Employment Applications," and you see that it is empty. After 15 minutes of searching, you find the applications in your assistant's drawer. You begin the first interview 10 minutes late.

3. A fax arrives at 4:30 P.M. from a client requesting some important information needed by 9:00 the next morning. You must leave for a meeting outside the office right then, and you ask your assistant to complete the assignment before leaving for the day. You explain the urgency of the task and she agrees to stay until it is done. When you arrive the next morning at 8:30 A.M., you find a note from your assistant that says, "Sorry, I couldn't find the information you wanted." You hurriedly find the needed information and fax it to the client. Your assistant arrives at her desk at her scheduled starting time of 9:00 A.M.

Situation #1

1. *Describe the situation.*

    I would say:

    _____

    _____

    _____

    _____

2. *Ask the employee for his or her view of the situation.*

    I would say:

    _____

    _____

    _____

    _____

3. *Come to an understanding of the situation.*

   I would say:

   _____

   _____

   _____

   _____

4. *Develop an action plan to take to resolve the situation.*

   I would say:

   _____

   _____

   _____

   _____

5. *Agree to follow up later to make certain the situation has been resolved.*

   I would say:

   _____

   _____

   _____

   _____

Situation #2

1. *Describe the situation.*

   I would say:

   _____

   _____

   _____

   _____

2. *Ask the employee for his or her view of the situation.*

   I would say:

   _____

   _____

   _____

   _____

3. *Come to an understanding of the situation.*

    I would say:

    _____

    _____

    _____

    _____

4. *Develop an action plan to take to resolve the situation.*

    I would say:

    _____

    _____

    _____

    _____

5. *Agree to follow up later to make certain the situation has been resolved.*

    I would say:

    _____

    _____

    _____

    _____

Situation #3

1. *Describe the situation.*

    I would say:

    _____

    _____

    _____

    _____

2. *Ask the employee for his or her view of the situation.*

    I would say:

    _____

    _____

    _____

    _____

3. *Come to an understanding of the situation.*

   I would say:

   _____

   _____

   _____

   _____

4. *Develop an action plan to take to resolve the situation.*

   I would say:

   _____

   _____

   _____

   _____

5. *Agree to follow up later to make certain the situation has been resolved.*

   I would say:

   _____

   _____

   _____

   _____

Read each of the following three situations. We will need one participant to volunteer to play the role of the supervisor for each situation, and another to play the role of employee. The remaining participants are observers.

Supervisors: Write what you would say for each of the five steps. Use the worksheets on the following pages to write your script for each situation.

Observers: Use the worksheets on the following pages to write down what the supervisor says to demonstrate each step. When the role-play is complete, use your notes to give the supervisor feedback.

1. You asked an employee to straighten up the waiting room before leaving for the day. She has done this job before, so you didn't go over each specific task with her. When you arrive at work the next morning, you see that she did a sloppy job. She left one of the wastebaskets half-filled with trash, didn't rinse out the coffeepot, and stacked up the magazines instead of neatly fanning them out on the coffee table.

2. You ask the new administrative assistant to pack up three orders for shipping. You have showed her before how to fill out the Fed Ex airbill and even have a sample filled out and placed on the bulletin board. At the end of the day, another employee brings you the packages and shows you that the airbills for all three orders are only partially filled out. The information on the left side has not been completed.

3. Your new employee has been 20 minutes late three times in two weeks.

Situation #1

1. *Describe the situation.*

_____

_____

_____

_____

2. *Ask the employee for his or her view of the situation.*

_____

_____

_____

_____

3. *Come to an understanding of the situation.*

_____

_____

_____

_____

4. *Develop an action plan to take to resolve the situation.*

_____

_____

_____

_____

5. *Agree to follow up later to make certain the situation has been resolved.*

_____

_____

_____

_____

Situation #2

1. *Describe the situation.*

_____

_____

_____

_____

2. *Ask the employee for his or her view of the situation.*

_____

_____

_____

_____

3. *Come to an understanding of the situation.*

_____

_____

_____

_____

4. *Develop an action plan to take to resolve the situation.*

_____

_____

_____

_____

5. *Agree to follow up later to make certain the situation has been resolved.*

_____

_____

_____

_____

Situation #3

1. *Describe the situation.*

_____

_____

_____

_____

2. *Ask the employee for his or her view of the situation.*

_____

_____

_____

_____

3. *Come to an understanding of the situation.*

_____

_____

_____

_____

4. *Develop an action plan to take to resolve the situation.*

_____

_____

_____

_____

5. *Agree to follow up later to make certain the situation has been resolved.*

_____

_____

_____

_____

Chapter 6

Balancing Work
and Family Life

Presentation Synopsis

In the aftermath of the downsized 1990s, most people report heavier workloads and increased expectations at work. It is becoming more and more difficult for many people to meet the obligations of both work and home. Through a series of exercises and group discussions, participants evaluate their own work/family situations, learning skills to simplify life and regain balance.

This presentation is based, in part, on information drawn from the following books. I recommend that you review them as you prepare your presentation.

Adams, Ramona, Herbert Otto, and Audeane Cowley. *Letting Go: Uncomplicating Your Life.* New York: Macmillan, 1980.

Carter, Steven, and Julia Sokol. *Lives without Balance: When You're Giving Everything You've Got and Still Not Getting What You Hoped For.* New York: Villard Books, 1992.

Eyre, Linda and Richard Eyre. *Lifebalance: How to Simplify and Bring Harmony to Your Everyday Life.* New York: Fireside, 1987.

Fassel, Diane. *Working Ourselves to Death: The High Cost of Workaholism and the Rewards of Recovery.* New York: HarperCollins, 1990.

Hunter, Marlene. *Creative Scripts for Hypnotherapy.* New York: Brunner/Mazel, 1994.

Koch, Richard. *The 80/20 Principle: The Secret of Achieving More with Less.* New York: Currency Books, 1998.

Time Requirements

This presentation runs approximately 1½ hours, depending on the style of the presenter.

🕐 **Clock symbol.** This means that the information is included for a longer seminar or workshop. Omit these sections for a shorter presentation. If time is limited, another way to shorten your presentation is to share the information in lecture format. However, keep in mind that it is often harder to engage and maintain the audience's interest with pure lecture style. Unless you are a particularly dynamic speaker, you will probably want to keep at least a few of the exercises to enliven the presentation.

Supplies needed. Outline, handouts, markers, masking tape, business cards, practice brochure, visual aids (slides, transparencies, or posters). This workshop also requires a tape or CD of classical music and a player.

Video examples. You may wish to show relevant short segments of popular movies to set the mood, stimulate discussion, or illustrate certain points. Look for relevant scenes in movies such as *How Stella Got Her Groove Back, City Slickers, Wall Street, Broadcast News, Lost in America, Grand Canyon,* and *Defending Your Life.* Some of these are noted in the outline.

If you plan to use videos to illustrate any points, have them cued up before your participants arrive. Make certain you know how to operate all audiovisual equipment before you begin your presentation. Murphy's Law seems to be in action when we are presenting workshops.

How to Use This Presentation

Possible Audiences	Whom to Contact
Businesspeople	Company presidents, human resources managers or other executives; Chamber of Commerce, Rotary, and similar business groups
Adult education groups at churches and synagogues	Director of adult education programs
Women's civic and professional organizations	Director of educational programs

Sample Text for Marketing Letter, Brochure, or Postcard

In the aftermath of the downsized 1990s, most people feel overloaded at their workplaces these days. It is becoming more and more difficult for most of us to meet the obligations of both work and home. To help you find ways to cope, _____ is offering an educational and motivational seminar to your group/company as a community service. Through a series of group activities, written exercises, and group discussion, this workshop helps participants assess the degree of balance in their own lives and identify strategies for creating more of it.

_____ is a licensed _____ in private practice in _____. S/he specializes in _____ and _____. Call _____ today to schedule your group's **free** workshop. (_____) _____-_____.

Sample Text for Press Release

_____ Presents "Balancing Work and Family" Workshop

_____ is presenting a **free** workshop on how to restore the balance between work and family life. The workshop is scheduled for _____, from _____ to _____ at _____. The workshop is limited to ____ participants and is open to the public.

According to _____, "Many people today are having a hard time balancing work and family responsibilities. The 1990s wave of downsizing has left most companies short-staffed, and people are expected to do more. Yet they still have family obligations and need some private time. This workshop is about finding ways to restore that balance."

_____ is a licensed _____ in private practice in _____. S/he specializes in _____ and _____. For reservations, call _____ at (_____) _____-_____.

Exhibit 6.1   Presentation Outline

Balancing Work and Family Life

Topic	*Time Estimate*
I. Introduction	
A. Introduce yourself	1 minute
B. Ask group members to introduce themselves	10 minutes
C. State workshop goals	1 minute
II. Exploring balance and success	13 minutes
III. Life triangle	5 minutes
IV. 80/20 rule	5 minutes
V. Your top 20	25 minutes
VI. Five relationship ingredients	7 minutes
VII. Your seven habits of success	22 minutes
VIII. Dealing with workaholism	7 minutes
IX. Visualization	3 minutes
X. Conclusion	1 minute
Approximate total time	**90–100 minutes**

Exhibit 6.2   Presentation Script

Balancing Work and Family Life

Outline	Presenter's Comments	Activity
I-A. **Introduce Yourself**	My name is _____. I'm a licensed _____, with a _____. I specialize in working with _____. For many years, I have worked with lots of clients who face the challenges of juggling work and family responsibilities. This balancing act is a challenge for many people today, and I think I have learned some things that might help you in your own life.	Refer to your bio on the first page of the handouts.
I-B. **Group Intro** ⏱	I'd like to begin today's workshop by learning a few things about each of you. Let's go around the room and each of you give your name and tell us where you work and what you do there.	If the group is under 20 people, ask participants to introduce themselves.
I-C. **Goals**	In today's workshop, you will have an opportunity to examine the balance of your own work/family situation. You will work on some exercises and participate in discussions that will help you begin to simplify your life and restore a sense of balance.	State goals.
II. **Exploring Balance and Success** **Video Illustration**	To illustrate what a *lack* of balance looks like, I'd like to show a scene from the opening moments of the 1998 movie *How Stella Got Her Groove Back. (Show the scene where Angela Bassett is on several phone calls at once before she leaves for her vacation. Alternatives include a scene from* Wall Street *or the "passing the tape" scene from* Broadcast News.*)*	Show video. 1 minute. Lead discussion. 1 minute.
	Does this look familiar? I hope not—it's meant to illustrate an extreme situation.	
	Now that we know what a life out of balance looks like, let's take a moment to think about the meaning of success.	
	Please complete Handout 6.1. Follow the instructions at the top. Give yourself 7 to 10 minutes to work on this.	Handout 6.1. Complete handout. 10 minutes.
	Next I'd like two or three of you to share your conclusions and observations from this exercise.	Lead discussion. 3 minutes.
	Once you have a perspective on what success can look like (that it's more than just making money or getting promoted), it's important to have some tools for keeping that perspective.	

Outline	Presenter's Comments	Activity
III. **Life Triangle**	In *Lifebalance*, authors Linda and Richard Eyre use a triangle to illustrate how to maintain a balance in your life so you have time and energy for your work, your family, and yourself.	Present information. 5 minutes.
	Handout 6.2 shows a triangle that represents these three parts of your life: self, work, and family.	Handout 6.2.
	According to *Lifebalance,* "Each of the three corners balances the other two, supports the other two, and draws from the other two. The way we build and develop and enjoy ourselves is through our work and our families. We try to teach families the work and skills of achievement and the respect of self and individuality. And our work and careers are for our families and the fulfillment of self and contributions to others. *The danger lies not so much in forgetting that all three are important but in letting other, less important things get ahead of them or in allowing them to get out of balance with each other*" (page 89; italics added).	
	What is the danger of focusing too much on family?	Lead discussion.

Answer to look for:

Work and self get neglected.

What is the danger of focusing too much on work?

Answer to look for:

Family and self get neglected.

What is the danger of focusing too much on the self?

Answer to look for:

Work and family get neglected.

Authors Linda and Richard Eyre suggest that you begin the habit of daily balancing. They recommend setting one priority each day for each corner of the triangle. Write the three priorities down before you do any other planning or scheduling of your day.

What are a few examples of priorities for each corner of the triangle?

Outline	Presenter's Comments	Activity

Possible answers:

- *Work:* Finish Project X, set up interviews, complete filing, and so on.
- *Family:* Spend 20 minutes reading to Mary, play Scrabble with husband and daughter after dinner, and so on.
- *Self:* Read one chapter in new novel, write in journal for 30 minutes, walk around the lake after dinner.

**IV.
80/20 Rule**

The 80/20 Rule (also known as the Pareto Principle) says that 20 percent of what we do produces 80 percent of the results.

Activity: Handout 6.3.
Present information.

Handout 6.3 shows a diagram of this concept. Some examples of this principle are:

- 20 percent of the people sell 80 percent of the widgets.
- 20 percent of the salespeople earn 80 percent of the commission.
- 20 percent of the parts in your car cause 80 percent of the breakdowns.
- 20 percent of the members of an organization do 80 percent of the work.

I'd like to hear a few more examples.

Why is this important and what does it have to do with balancing work and family?

Activity: Ask for examples.
5 minutes.
Lead discussion.

Answer to look for:

The 80/20 principle can help anyone have more happiness and and achieve more. Here's how:

1. Identify the times when you are *most* happy and productive (i.e., the 20 percent that produces the 80 percent) and *expand* them as much as possible.

2. Identify the times when you are *least* happy and productive (i.e., the 80 percent that produces the 20 percent), and *reduce* them as much as possible.

**V.
Your Top 20**

Handout 6.4 will help you apply the 80/20 principle to your relationships. Ask participants to complete the "Your Top 20" exercise. Allow 20 minutes. If time is too short, you may want to suggest that participants complete this exercise on their own later.

Activity: Handout 6.4.
Individual exercise.
20 minutes.

Outline	Presenter's Comments	Activity
	I'd like to hear your observations. Where did your partner come up on the list? Above or below your parents or children? Many people find that they spend much less than 80 percent of the time with the few people who produce 80 percent of the "relationship value" to you.	Lead group discussion. 5 minutes.
	What are the implications of this concept for you?	

Answer to look for:

Your goal should be to go for quality rather than quantity. Spend your time and emotional energy reinforcing the relationships that are the most important.

Outline	Presenter's Comments	Activity
VI. **Five Relationship Ingredients**	Richard Koch describes a "five ingredient" relationship. Participants may take notes on Handout 6.5. The best relationships include these five ingredients:	Handout 6.5. Present information.
	1. Mutual enjoyment 2. Mutual respect 3. Shared experience 4. Reciprocity 5. Trust	
	Please complete the exercise individually. Give yourself about five minutes.	Individual exercise. 5 minutes.
	Now that you are finished with the exercise, I'd like one or two people to share their observations.	Lead group discussion. 2 minutes.
	Think about the people you spend time with socially, but basically for professional purposes. How many of them do you really like? Lots of people spend a lot of time with people they really don't like. This is not a good use of your time. It's not fun, it makes you tired, and, often, it's expensive. *It keeps you from doing better things.*	
	You might want to give yourself permission to stop doing it—and, instead, spend more time with the people you enjoy and who make you a better person.	
VII. **Your Seven Habits of Success**	You have probably heard of Stephen Covey's "Seven Habits of Highly Effective People." In this next exercise, I'd like you to design your own list of success habits. What seven things would lead to more happiness in your life if you did them every day?	Handout 6.6. Individual exercise. 5 minutes.
	Think about this and list them on Handout 6.6. Give yourself 3 to 5 minutes.	

Outline	Presenter's Comments	Activity
	Now I'd like to form groups of three and make a group list that combines your individual lists. Give yourselves about five minutes.	Small group exercise. 5 minutes.
	Let's take a few minutes and have each group report on their seven habits. I will record your ideas on the easel, creating a master list for the entire group.	Lead group discussion; post ideas on easel pad. 7 minutes.
	In *The 80/20 Principle,* author Koch lists these seven habits: 1. Get some physical exercise. 2. Stimulate yourself mentally (read, do puzzles, discuss, or write for 20 minutes). 3. Stimulate yourself artistically or spiritually (read, see a movie, watch the sunrise or sunset, look at the stars, go to a ball game or interesting meeting, meditate). 4. Do something for someone else. 5. Take a pleasure break with a friend. 6. Give yourself a treat. 7. Congratulate yourself on something you achieved today or on living in a worthwhile way.	Present information. Comment on similarities and differences. 5 minutes.
VIII. **Dealing with Workaholism**	What if a person needs more than just self-help to deal with a lack of balance in work and family life? An organization called Workaholics Anonymous can help.	Present information. 2 minutes.
	Workaholics Anonymous is a 12-step recovery program similar to Alcoholics Anonymous. It is a "fellowship of individuals who share their experience, strength and hope with each other that they may solve their common problem and help others recover from workaholism. The only requirement for membership is a desire to stop working compulsively." *(This information is available on the WA web site at* www.ai.mit.edu/people/wa.home.html.*)*	
	Handout 6.7 outlines a list titled "How Do You Know If You Are a Workaholic?" These 20 items can help any person identify whether their lack of balance in life is serious enough to be labeled "workaholism." Take a moment to read through this handout. Which items stand out for you? The 12 steps of Workaholics Anonymous and the Workaholics Anonymous recovery tools are powerful ways to obtain support for a life out of balance. Groups are available in most cities.	Handout 6.7. Read through list together and lead discussion. 5 minutes.

Outline	Presenter's Comments	Activity
IX. **Visualization**	I'd like to close this presentation with a visualization. *(You may also wish to substitute your own favorite visualization. Consider playing soft classical music in the background as you read.)*	Read visualization. 3 minutes.

Sit comfortably in your chair, uncross your arms and legs, and let your eyes close.

Take a long, slow, deep breath as you let your eyes close. Imagine yourself in a beautiful meadow. It is a golden summer day. The sky is a deep blue and there is a soft, gentle breeze. The sun is warm on your skin. You are sitting in a comfortable lawn chair and you hear the wind softly rustling the leaves of the trees.

You look on the edge of the meadow and see a grove of trees. You stand up and walk toward these beautiful trees and notice the many shades of green. When you get closer to the trees, you notice something you hadn't seen at first—a small creek, winding across the meadow.

You look around and find a small bridge crossing the creek. You cross over it easily and wander into the grove of trees. The sunlight filters through the branches and makes dancing patterns on your path. On the floor of the grove, tiny purple flowers and ivy make a beautiful carpet. You see a squirrel run up a tree and hear a bird chirping softly. As you walk, you are filled with feelings of serenity and peace. You wander along, feeling calm and comforted. This serene place somehow also makes you feel strong and powerful.

You come to a large boulder that is shaped just like a chair. You decide to sit down for a few moments and enjoy the peace you are feeling. You just sit for a while and listen to the birds.

(Pause for a minute.)

You become aware of your breathing and feel at one with nature.

After a few moments of sitting on the boulder, you stand up and begin to walk again. You come to the edge of the grove. You see the meadow where you came from and the bridge. You walk back toward it. You cross the bridge and go back to the place where you started.

(Pause)

In a moment, I will ask you to open your eyes. Become aware of the room where you are sitting, and feel yourself

Outline	Presenter's Comments	Activity
	sitting in your chair. Begin to move your feet, and your legs, and your arms. When you are ready, open your eyes.	
	(This visualization is adapted from one found in Creative Scripts for Hypnotherapy; *see information at the beginning of this chapter.)*	
X. **Conclusion**	I hope you have enjoyed today's workshop. In the time remaining, I would be happy to answer any questions you may have.	Conclude the workshop.

Handout 6.1 What Is Your Definition of Success?

The purpose of this exercise is for you to create your own definition of success. The following items are a place to start; please add your own. Which items are the most fundamental to your success definition? Which items represent the greatest challenge to you?

1. I set aside time to do things that are fun.

2. I take care of my spirit.

3. I know what I value and live my life accordingly.

4. I put my best efforts into things.

5. I take charge of my situation and make changes when I'm not satisfied with how things are going.

6. When something doesn't work out, I know when to move on without regret.

7. I consciously look for ways to bring out my creativity.

8. I am comfortable being myself.

9. I am doing what I love today. I am not waiting for "someday."

10. I know my strengths and give myself credit for what I do well.

11. I spend time with the people I love.

12. I take good care of my body.

13. I manage my money responsibly.

Add your own items: _____

_____

_____

_____

The most important items to me are: _____

_____

_____

_____

My greatest challenges are: _____

_____

_____

_____

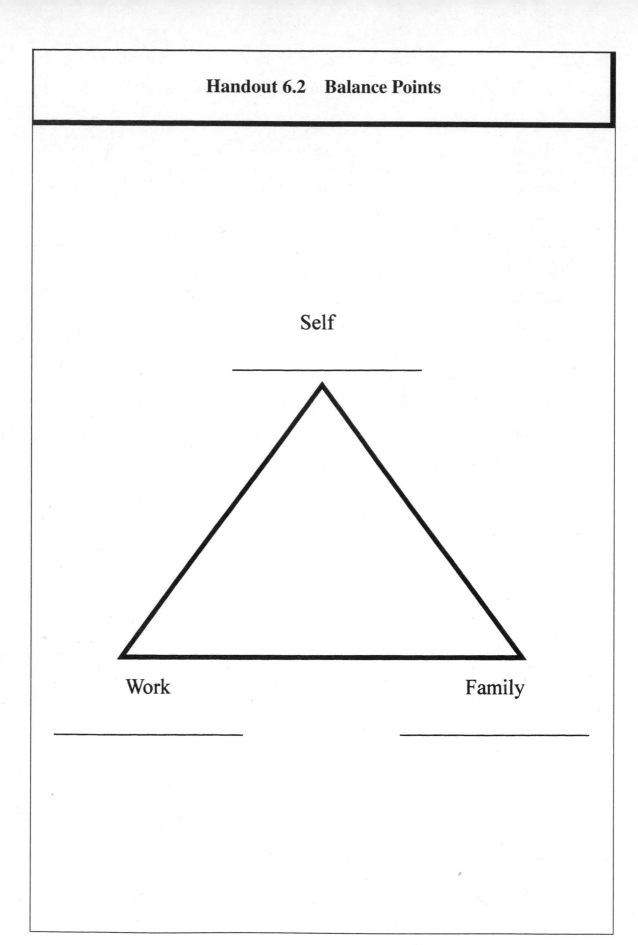

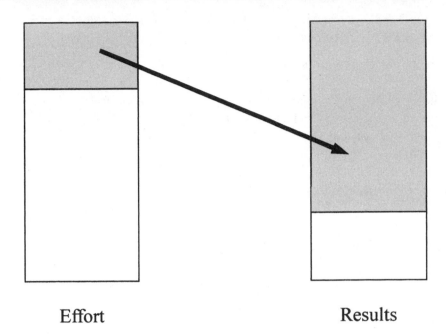

Effort   Results

There are only a few things that ever produce important results. Maximize the *vital few* and mini-mize the *trivial many*. Here are some ways:

- Aggressively pursue the 20-percent activities—those that give you 80 percent of your happiness and productivity.

- Spend your time with 20-percent people—those who make you feel good about yourself.

- Avoid the 80-percent people, places, and activities; they prevent you from spending time in the vital 20 percent.

Handout 6.4   Your Top 20

Under "My Top 20," list the names of your Top 20 people: friends and loved ones with whom you have your most important relationships.

1. List them in order from most important to least important.

2. Decide how important each relationship is by thinking about how trusting, close, and intimate it is. Think about the extent to which each relationship helps you in life and how much it makes you a better person.

3. Next, assign a total of 100 points among the relationships in terms of their importance to you. You may need to spend some time working on the numbers to make them add up to 100.

4. Finally, assign a total of 100 points among the relationships in terms of the amount of time you spend with each person. Again, you may need to work on the numbers to make them add up to 100.

My Top 20

Rank	Name	Points	Time
1.	_____	____	____
2.	_____	____	____
3.	_____	____	____
4.	_____	____	____
5.	_____	____	____
6.	_____	____	____
7.	_____	____	____
8.	_____	____	____
9.	_____	____	____
10.	_____	____	____
11.	_____	____	____

Rank	Name		Points	Time
12.	_____		_____	_____
13.	_____		_____	_____
14.	_____		_____	_____
15.	_____		_____	_____
16.	_____		_____	_____
17.	_____		_____	_____
18.	_____		_____	_____
19.	_____		_____	_____
20.	_____		_____	_____

Handout 6.5   Great Relationships: Five Ingredients

1. _____

2. _____

3. _____

4. _____

5. _____

For each of the following categories, note two or three relationships that embody the five ingredients. You may wish to add or change one or two categories, depending on your life situation.

Personal

_____

_____

_____

Professional—Peers

_____

_____

_____

Professional—Mentors

_____

_____

_____

Professional—Protégés

_____

_____

_____

Handout 6.6   Seven Daily Habits

List seven habits that, if performed daily, would lead to more happiness in your life.

1. _____

2. _____

3. _____

4. _____

5. _____

6. _____

7. _____

Handout 6.7 How Do You Know If You Are a Workaholic?

Workaholics Anonymous suggests that you ask yourself these questions:

1. Do you get more excited about your work than about family or anything else?
2. Are there times when you can charge through your work and other times when you can't?
3. Do you take work with you to bed? On weekends? On vacation?
4. Is work the activity you like to do best and talk about most?
5. Do you work more than 40 hours a week?
6. Do you turn your hobbies into moneymaking ventures?
7. Do you take complete responsibility for the outcome of your work efforts?
8. Have your family or friends given up expecting you on time?
9. Do you take on extra work because you are concerned that it won't otherwise get done?
10. Do you underestimate how long a project will take and then rush to complete it?
11. Do you believe that it is okay to work long hours if you love what you are doing?
12. Do you get impatient with people who have other priorities besides work?
13. Are you afraid that if you don't work hard you will lose your job or be a failure?
14. Is the future a constant worry for you even when things are going very well?
15. Do you do things energetically and competitively, including play?
16. Do you get irritated when people ask you to stop doing your work in order to do something else?
17. Have your long hours hurt your family or other relationships?
18. Do you think about your work while driving or falling asleep, or when others are talking?
19. Do you work or read during meals?
20. Do you believe that more money will solve the other problems in your life?

The 12 Steps of Workaholics Anonymous

1. We admitted we were powerless over our compulsive working—that our lives had become unmanageable.
2. Came to believe that a Power greater than ourselves could restore us to sanity.
3. Made a decision to turn our will and our lives over to the care of God *as we understood Him.*
4. Made a searching and fearless moral inventory of ourselves.
5. Admitted to God, to ourselves, and to another human being the exact nature of our wrongs.

6. Were entirely ready to have God remove all these defects of character.

7. Humbly asked Him to remove our shortcomings.

8. Made a list of all persons we had harmed, and became willing to make amends to them all.

9. Made direct amends to such people wherever possible, except when to do so would injure them or others.

10. Continued to take personal inventory, and when we were wrong promptly admitted it.

11. Sought through prayer and meditation to improve our conscious contact with God as we understood Him, praying only for the knowledge of His will for us and the power to carry that out.

12. Having had a spiritual awakening as the result of these steps, we tried to carry this message to workaholics and to practice these principles in all our affairs.

Note: The 12 Steps of Workaholics Anonymous, as adapted by Workaholics Anonymous with permission of Alcoholics Anonymous World Services, Inc. (AAWS) are printed with permission of Workaholics Anonymous and AAWS. Permission to adapt and reprint the 12 Steps does not mean that AA has reviewed or approved the contents of this publication, or that AA necessarily agrees with the views expressed herein. AA is a program of recovery from alcoholism *only;* use of the 12 Steps in connection with programs and activities which are patterned after AA, but which address other problems, or in any other non-AA context, does not imply otherwise.

Workaholics Anonymous Recovery Tools

Listening
We set aside time each day for prayer and meditation. Before accepting any commitments, we ask our Higher Power and friends for guidance.

Prioritizing
We decide which are the most important things to do first. Sometimes that may mean doing nothing. We strive to stay flexible to events, reorganizing our priorities as needed. We view interruptions and accidents as opportunities for growth.

Substituting
We do not add a new activity without eliminating from our schedule one that demands equivalent time and energy.

Underscheduling
We allow more time than we think we need for a task or trip, allowing a comfortable margin to accommodate the unexpected.

Playing
We schedule time for play, refusing to let ourselves work nonstop. We do not make our play into a work project.

Concentrating
We try to do one thing at a time.

Pacing

We work at a comfortable pace and rest before we get tired. To remind ourselves, we check our level of energy before proceeding to our next activity. We do not get wound up in our work, so we do not have to unwind.

Relaxing

We do not yield to pressure or attempt to pressure others. We remain alert to the people and situations that trigger pressure in us. We become aware of our own actions, words, body sensations, and feelings that tell us we're responding to pressure. When we feel tension, we stop to reconnect to our Higher Power and others around us.

Accepting

We accept the outcomes of our endeavors, whatever the results, whatever the timing. We know that impatience, rushing, and insisting on perfect results only slow down our recovery. We are gentle with our efforts, knowing that our new way of living requires much practice.

Asking

We admit our weaknesses and mistakes, and ask our Higher Power and others for help.

Meetings

We attend WA meetings to learn how the fellowship works and to share our experience, strength, and hope with each other.

Telephoning

We use the phone to stay in contact with other members of the fellowship between meetings. We communicate with our WA friends before and after a critical task.

Balancing

We balance our work involvement with efforts to develop personal relationships, spiritual growth, creativity, and playful attitudes.

Serving

We readily extend help to other workaholics, knowing that assistance to others adds to the quality of our own recovery.

Living in the Now

We realize we are where our Higher Power wants us to be—in the here and now. We try to live each moment with serenity, joy, and gratitude.

For more information about Workaholics Anonymous, write or call:

Workaholics Anonymous
World Service Organization
P.O. Box 289
Menlo Park, CA 94026-0289 USA
(510) 273-925

Source: Unofficial web site of Workaholics Anonymous, www.ai.mit.edu/people/wa.home.html.

Chapter 7

How to Recover from
a Career Crash

Presentation Synopsis

This presentation focuses on what a career crash is, its common causes, and why a career crash is so devastating. You will help participants understand who is hurt the most by a career crash and how people recover. Other topics include how to help a career crash survivor and how to turn a crash into a victory.

This presentation is based, in part, on information drawn from the following books. I recommend that you review them as you prepare your presentation.

Bridges, William. *Job Shift: How to Prosper in a Workplace without Jobs.* Reading, MA: Addison-Wesley, 1994.

Glassner, Barry. *Career Crash: The New Crisis—and Who Survives.* New York: Simon & Schuster, 1994.

Pines, Ayala, and Elliot Aronson. *Career Burnout: Causes and Cures.* New York: Free Press, 1988.

Time Requirements

This presentation runs from 1 hour to 1½ hours, depending on the style of the presenter and the number of interactive activities used.

🕐 **Clock symbol.** This means that the information is included for a longer seminar or workshop. Omit these sections for a shorter presentation. If time is limited, another way to shorten your presentation is to share the information in lecture format. However, keep in mind that it is often harder to engage and maintain the audience's interest with pure lecture style. Unless you are a particularly dynamic speaker, you will probably want to keep at least a few of the exercises to enliven the presentation.

Video examples. Showing selected scenes from popular movies is one way to make your presentation more interesting. It creates some variety and interest, stimulates discussion, and might be a way to inject some humor. Consider selecting short scenes from videos such as *Jerry Maguire, The Full Monty,* and *Lost in America.* Suggestions for specific scenes are included in this outline, but you are encouraged to look for other examples on your own as you prepare for your presentation.

How to Use This Presentation

Possible Audiences	Whom to Contact
Adult education groups at churches and synagogues	Director of adult education programs
PTO/PTA	PTO/PTA president
Women's civic and professional organizations	Director of educational programs
Businesspeople	Director of educational programs; Chamber of Commerce, Rotary, other business groups

Sample Text for Marketing Letter, Brochure, or Postcard

Would the members of your organization enjoy a personal growth workshop? _____ is offering "How to Recover from a Career Crash," an educational and motivational seminar, to your group as a community service.

This presentation focuses on what a career crash is, its common causes, and why a career crash is so devastating. You will help participants understand who is hurt the most by a career crash and how people recover. Other topics include how to help a career crash survivor and how to turn a crash into a victory.

_____ is a licensed _____ in private practice in _____. S/he specializes in _____ and _____. Call _____ today to schedule your group's **free** workshop. (_____) _____-_____.

Sample Text for Press Release

_____ Presents "How to Recover from a Career Crash"

_____ is presenting a **free** workshop on how to recover from a career crash. The workshop is scheduled for _____, from _____ to _____ at _____. The workshop is limited to _____ participants and is open to the public.

According to _____, "A career crash is any experience where your career is in crisis: being fired, laid off, demoted, or stuck in a job where you hate going to work in the morning. A career crash can be devastating to the person going through it as well as the people around him or her. It can feel like a significant loss and cause the same kinds of symptoms as other kinds of losses." In this workshop, participants will learn how people recover from career crises, how to help a career crash survivor, and how to turn a crash into a victory.

_____ is a licensed _____ in private practice in _____. S/he specializes in _____ and _____. For reservations, call _____ at (_____) _____-_____.

Exhibit 7.1   Presentation Outline

How to Recover from a Career Crash

Topic	*Time Estimate*
I. Introduction	
A. Introduce yourself	1 minute
B. Ask group members to introduce themselves	10 minutes
C. State workshop goals	1 minute
II. What is a career crash?	2–3 minutes
Video example	
III. Common causes of career crashes	2–7 minutes
IV. Why a career crash is so devastating	6–14 minutes
Video examples	
V. Career crash: who it hurts the most	1 minute
VI. The flashback effect	2–4 minutes
VII. Stages of recovery	12 minutes
VIII. How to help a career crash survivor	5–7 minutes
IX. How to turn a crash into a victory	20–30 minutes
X. Conclusion	
Approximate total time	**52–90 minutes**

Exhibit 7.2   Presentation Script

How to Recover from a Career Crash

Outline	Presenter's Comments	Activity
I-A. **Introduce Yourself**	My name is _____. I'm a licensed _____, with a _____, and became interested in how to help people deal with major career disruptions when _____ _____.	Refer to your bio on the first page of the handouts. 1 minute.
I-B. **Group Intro** ☺	I'd like to begin today's workshop by finding out a bit about each of you. Let's go around the room and each person introduce yourself and tell us what brings you to this workshop.	If the group is under 20 people, ask participants to introduce themselves. 10 minutes.
I-C. **Goals**	In this workshop, we will explore what happens when a person has a "career crash" and what can be done about it. We will look at common causes of career crashes, how they affect people, how to recover, and even how to turn the experience into a victory. The workshop is structured with lectures, group discussions, and a few video scenes that will illustrate some of the points. *Begin by stating relevant statistics or facts about recent events at local companies. For example, a large company may recently have closed a plant and laid off hundreds of people, or a recent newspaper article may have cited some surprising statistics about current employment trends.*	State goals. 1 minute. 2 minutes.
II. **What Is a Career Crash?** ☺	You may wish to take some notes on Handout 7.1 as we discuss this topic. How would you define a career crash?	Handout 7.1. Lead discussion. 2 minutes.

Answers to look for:

- Losing your job
- Being fired
- Burning out
- Not wanting to do your job for one more day

A career crash can be caused either by someone else (being laid off) or by your own feelings (burning out). Here is a good example.

Outline	Presenter's Comments	Activity
Video Example	*(Show the scene from the movie* Jerry Maguire *where Jerry [Tom Cruise] is fired at the restaurant.)*	Show video. 1 minute.
III. Common Causes of Career Crashes ⏱	There are many reasons why people experience a career crash. Here are a few: • Corporate downsizing • Burnout • Moving because of spouse's career • Being fired • Making the wrong career move • Corporate politics • Making one faux pas too many What are some other reasons for career crashes? Which of these causes apply to you?	Present information. 2 minutes. List responses on easel. 5 minutes. Encourage discussion if time allows.

IV. Why a Career Crash Is So Devastating	Crashes are almost always devastating. Some of the reasons behind them are the following. *(Note your own examples to illustrate some of these points.)*
	
	1. *Money:* Losing your only source of income with no warning is financially devastating.
	
	2. *Status:* If a job conveys status and provides an identity, you will be devastated when the job is taken away.
	
	3. *Surprise:* If the job loss happens without warning, such a loss is shocking.
	
	4. *Multiple losses:*
	
	  • Loss of self-esteem; feelings of shame and embarrassment are normal.
	  • Loss of friends and companions.
	  • Loss of a regular schedule or routine.
		Present information. 6 minutes.

⏱ **Video Example**	In the 1997 film *The Full Monty*, actor Tom Wilkinson plays Gerald, who has been unemployed and a regular at the Job Club for six months. He hasn't yet had the courage to tell his wife that he has lost his job. *(Show any scene that illustrates Gerald's feelings of embarrassment.)* 5. *Confusion:* If the crash happens because of burnout or for reasons within yourself, you are likely to feel very confused about what to do next.	Show video. 2 minutes. Present information.

Outline	Presenter's Comments	Activity
	6. *Effect on others:* If people around you depend on your income and need you to be predictable, they may have their own negative reactions to your crash.	
⏱ **Video Example**	*(Show the scene from the 1985 movie* Lost in America *where Julie Hagerty, who plays the wife of Albert Brooks, gambles away the couple's money after they have both quit their jobs.)*	Show video. 2 minutes. Lead discussion. 1 minute.
⏱	What other kinds of negative or strange reactions have you experienced or heard of? What are some other reasons that a crash is devastating?	List ideas on easel. 1 minute. Encourage group to share experiences as time allows. 2 minutes.
V. Career Crash: Who It Hurts the Most	A career crash hurts *you* because it is devastating to your ego. The hurt tends to be greater when one gets a sense of identity and self-esteem from his or her job title, status, and income. A crash hurts *your family* because they must experience the emotional fallout that follows a crash. The family may also experience a feeling of lost self-esteem and status, especially if the crash victim was fired or laid off.	Present information. 1 minute.
VI. The Flashback Effect	A major loss like this sometimes can reach back into the past and reactivate unfinished business that may be left over from a major loss or disappointment from an earlier time. For example, when Sharon was terminated after seven months at her dream job, she became very depressed. While depression is a normal reaction to such a loss, Sharon was reacting to losing her job *and* to the similar feelings she had when she flunked out of a top university 12 years earlier. When she finally saw a therapist after a few weeks of depression following the job loss, she saw that she had never fully resolved her feelings about failing in college.	Present information. 2 minutes. Lead discussion. 2 minutes.
⏱	Would anyone like to share a similar example?	
VII. Stages of Recovery	The human response to loss is almost always the same. Dr. Elisabeth Kübler-Ross described five stages of grieving, and these stages have been found in response to just about any kind of loss.	Present information. 5 minutes.

Outline	Presenter's Comments	Activity

The stages are:

1. Denial (shock, numbness, withdrawal; "I can't believe it")

2. Anger ("Those jerks!" and "I'm so stupid!")

3. Bargaining ("Please, God" and "Give me just one more chance")

4. Depression (signs include sleeping, eating, sadness, crying)

5. Acceptance (when you are ready to move on)

People usually go through all five stages of grief, although the stages may occur in a different order.

Who would like to share what you remember of your own stages of recovery?

Lead discussion as time allows.

3 minutes.

Here are some other points about recovery:

Present information.

4 minutes.

1. The process of recovering from a career crash will happen on its own schedule. It can't be rushed.

2. Every person responds to a career crash differently. There is no right way to respond or to deal with it.

3. Depending on the circumstances, processing a career crash can take years.

4. Build and use a support system. People need other people when they are experiencing such a crisis. A group of people who have experienced similar losses is especially helpful.

5. It is a good idea to find support outside of your family and friends. Even the most supportive may grow tired of hearing about your situation, or you may find yourself censoring your behavior to avoid alienating them. However, you still need help and a place to let your feelings out.

VIII. How to Help a Career Crash Survivor

I'd like to offer a few ideas for being helpful to people going through career crises:

Present information.

Give your own examples of these points.

5 minutes.

1. People need support when they are having a career crash, even though they may seem to push you away.

2. Ask how you can help.

3. Don't give advice unless asked.

Outline	Presenter's Comments	Activity

4. Check in regularly with the crash victim; let him or her know you're there.

5. Remind the crash victim of what a good person he or she is, even without the identity and status that the job provided.

6. Sometimes a career crash sends a person into a serious depression for which help is needed. If you sense danger, urge the crash victim to seek help.

Who would like to suggest other ideas to add to this list?

Activity: Encourage discussion as time allows; list ideas on easel.

2 minutes.

**IX.
How to Turn a Crash into a Victory**

I have some suggestions for turning a career crash into a victory. Please feel free to share examples of these ideas as we discuss them.

Activity: Present information.

Give your own examples of these points.

5 minutes.

1. Give yourself time to heal. If recovery is rushed or interrupted, the crash victim will not fully heal and a victory is not possible.

2. Remind yourself as often as necessary that your pain will end and you will eventually feel happy again.

3. Avoid jumping into something new on the rebound; let yourself experience all the stages of grief.

4. Accept that many people will not understand the depth of your grief. They will not understand why this is so difficult for you and they will say stupid things.

5. Use the opportunity to stop and consider other options.

6. Explore what meaning your feelings have for you. If we pay attention to them, our feelings can lead us places we would otherwise never visit.

7. Keep a journal of your experiences. Make it your intention to see what there is to be learned from this experience.

8. A loss such as a career crash can be viewed as both a door-closer and a door-opener. Start thinking about what you are learning and gaining from this experience.

9. Create a ceremony of letting go. Yours will be as unique as your experience. Some examples:

- Have a funeral for the job or career you are letting go of. Maybe put some snapshots, memos, and other memorabilia in a shoe box and ceremonially bury it.

Outline	Presenter's Comments	Activity
🕐	• Write a press release announcing your new career step. Who would like to suggest other ideas to add to this list?	Encourage discussion as time allows; list ideas on easel. 5 minutes.
Career Crash Recovery Exercise	The Career Crash Recovery Exercise (Handout 7.2) will help you explore some of these ideas. Please take about 10 minutes to complete the exercise individually.	Handout 7.2. Complete exercise individually. 10 minutes.
🕐	Now please form groups of three or four and share one or two findings from this exercise. Take about 10 minutes. Now I'd like to have a few of you talk about your findings as you answered the questions on this handout.	Small group discussion if time allows. 10 minutes. Lead general discussion. 5 minutes.
IX. Conclusion	I hope you have enjoyed today's workshop. In the time remaining, I would be happy to answer any questions you may have.	Conclude the workshop.

Handout 7.1   Career Crash

1. What is a career crash?

   _____

   _____

2. What causes career crashes?

   _____

   _____

3. Why is a career crash so devastating?

   _____

   _____

4. Who hurts the most when there is a career crash?

   _____

   _____

5. What is the flashback effect?

   _____

   _____

6. Five stages of recovery:

   • _____

   • _____

   • _____

   • _____

   • _____

7. How to help a career crash survivor:

   _____

   _____

Handout 7.2   The Career Crash Recovery Exercise

1. Describe what happened when your career crashed.

   _____

   _____

2. Describe the job or career. Where did you work? What was it like? Who did you work with? What do you miss the most? What do you not miss at all?

   _____

   _____

   _____

   _____

   _____

3. Describe your feelings about the loss of the job or career.

   _____

   _____

4. What has the impact of this crash been on your life? What else have you lost because of your career crash?

   _____

   _____

   _____

5. Given what you have written, are your responses to this experience appropriate?

   _____

   _____

6. What barriers stop you from moving on?

_____

_____

7. What are 10 things you can do starting today to continue the recovery process?

- _____
- _____
- _____
- _____
- _____
- _____
- _____
- _____
- _____
- _____

Chapter 8

Does Your Company
Need Family Therapy?

Presentation Synopsis

In this workshop, participants learn how companies are like families. Topics include how family dynamics are brought into the workplace, signs of dysfunction, strategies for resolving problems, and what to do if the boss is the "problem patient." The workshop is a combination of lecture and group discussion.

This presentation is based, in part, on information drawn from the following books. I recommend that you review them as you prepare your presentation.

Nelson, Bob. *1001 Ways to Energize Employees.* New York: Workman, 1997.

Piercy, Fred, Douglas Sprenkle & Associates. *Family Therapy Sourcebook.* New York: Guilford Press, 1986.

Time Requirements

This presentation runs from ½ hour to 1½ hours, depending on the style of the presenter and the number of interactive activities used.

⏱ **Clock symbol.** This means that the information is included for a longer seminar or workshop. Omit these sections for a shorter presentation. If time is limited, another way to shorten your presentation is to share the information in lecture format. However, keep in mind that it is often harder to engage and maintain the audience's interest with pure lecture style. Unless you are a particularly dynamic speaker, you will probably want to keep at least a few of the exercises to enliven the presentation.

How to Use This Presentation

Possible Audiences	Whom to Contact
Businesspeople	Company presidents, human resources managers, or other executives; Chamber of Commerce, Rotary, and similar business groups
Adult education groups at churches and synagogues	Director of adult education programs
Women's civic and professional organizations	Director of educational programs

Sample Text for Marketing Letter, Brochure, or Postcard

Would the members of your organization enjoy a personal growth workshop? _____ is offering an educational and motivational seminar to your group as a community service.

In this workshop, participants learn how companies are like families. Topics include how family dynamics are brought into the workplace, signs of dysfunction, strategies for resolving problems, and what to do if the boss is the "problem patient." The workshop is a combination of lecture and group discussion.

_____ is a licensed _____ in private practice in _____. S/he specializes in _____ and _____. Call _____ today to schedule your group's **free** workshop. (_____) _____-_____.

Sample Text for Press Release

Does Your Company Need Family Therapy?

_____ is presenting a **free** workshop for anyone who works with other people. The workshop is scheduled for _____, from _____ to _____. The workshop is limited to ____ participants and is open to the public.

According to _____, "Every workplace is like a family. We all bring certain ways of relating to other people to the world of business; sometimes it's effective, and sometimes it creates problems for us. In this workshop, we'll look at how to tell if your work team is becoming dysfunctional, and we'll examine several strategies for creating improvement."

_____ is a licensed _____ in private practice in _____. S/he specializes in _____ and _____. For reservations, call _____ at (_____) _____-_____.

Exhibit 8.1 Presentation Outline

Does Your Company Need Family Therapy?

Topic	Time Estimate
I. **Introduction**	
A. Introduce yourself	1 minute
B. Ask group members to introduce themselves	10 minutes
C. State workshop goals	1 minute
II. **How companies are like families**	5–10 minutes
III. **Four dynamics that we bring to work from home**	6–12 minutes
IV. **Signs of dysfunction**	7–15 minutes
V. **Strategies for resolving problems**	10–15 minutes
VI. **What to do if the boss is the "problem patient"**	7–15 minutes
VII. **Conclusion**	
Approximate total time	**37–79 minutes**

Exhibit 8.2   Presentation Script

Does Your Company Need Family Therapy?

Outline	Presenter's Comments	Activity
I-A. **Introduce** **Yourself**	My name is _____. I'm a licensed _____, with a _____ degree in _____. I specialize in working with _____ and during the last few years have become interested in working with work groups within small and large companies. I have found that companies have many characteristics in common with families, and have learned to help work teams become more productive by applying some of the principles of family therapy.	Refer to your bio on the first page of the handouts. 1 minute.
I-B. **Group Intro** 🕐	I'd like to begin today's workshop by finding out a bit about each of you. Let's go around the room and each person tell us your name, where you work and two adjectives to describe your workplace.	10 minutes. Write adjectives on easel.
I-C. **Goals**	We will begin today's workshop by looking at how companies are like families. We will explore some of the signs that may indicate that the "work family" has become dysfunctional. We will also spend some time talking about some strategies for resolving problems in the workgroup. The workshop is structured with lectures and group discussions.	State goals. 1 minute.
II. **How** **Companies** **Are Like** **Families** 🕐	Like a family, a company is a group of people who have an ongoing relationship with one another. You may want to take notes on Handout 8.1. Think for a moment of some ways that companies are like families. What comes to mind?	_____

Answers to look for:

Companies have several things in common with families:

1. Families have distinct ways of communicating and degrees of togetherness. For example:

   - Overt versus covert communication
   - Enmeshed versus disengaged
   - Diffuse (extreme togetherness) versus rigid (extreme separateness) versus clear (ideal and appropriate) boundaries

2. There are unwritten rules that family members or employees must follow in order to survive and thrive in the system. For example, in an organization, the rules might be:

- Never call the boss by her first name.
- Always be at your desk by 8:00 A.M.
- Never eat lunch with a person of lower status.
- Don't place any personal items on your desk or credenza.

3. Unresolved issues from the past have an effect on current functioning and communication patterns.

Example: After an event such as the 1997 UPS strike, employees need time to process their feelings. Family therapy following a disruptive event like this would heal such wounds much more quickly.

Note your own example here: _____

_____

_____

_____

**III.
Four
Dynamics
That We
Bring to
Work from
Home**
🕐

We learn to relate to people first in our families of origin. We learn to trust, communicate, listen, cooperate, and share before we reach our tenth birthday. When we join a company, we bring those abilities with us. And every work team in every company becomes a place where family dynamics play themselves out, for better or worse.

Every member of every work team brings the following kinds of dynamics from home:

1. A preference for independence and autonomy versus dependence and control

    Example: Some people are most comfortable in a closely supervised work situation and prefer to have everything clearly spelled out. Others find such an atmosphere suffocating and seek an environment where they are left to their own devices.

2. The ability to recognize and respond to appropriate versus inappropriate boundaries

Present information.
6–12 minutes.

If time allows, ask for examples and encourage discussion.

Example: Some companies expect employees to demonstrate extreme loyalty and openness to those within the company. This atmosphere may feel comfortable to someone from a family with similar boundaries, inappropriate to another person.

3. The ability to communicate with others effectively:

    - Stating opinions and expectations overtly versus covertly
    - Demonstrating listening skills
    - Asking for clarification when needed
    - Speaking assertively
    - Showing respect for others

    Using effective communication skills requires strong self-esteem. This may be impossible for a person from a family where such communication was never modeled. A person who learned covert, aggressive, disrespectful communication patterns would not be successful in a work group where the behavior described in the preceding list is expected.

4. The ability to trust others

    How does the lack of trust in a work group lessen its effectiveness?

Answer to look for:

When employees do not trust one another, team functioning is threatened. Empowerment and motivation are maximized when people trust each other.

**IV.
Signs of
Dysfunction**
🕐

How can you tell if a work group (or a family) is not healthy? Here are some signs of dysfunction:

1. *Attendance:* Excessive absenteeism and high turnover are similar to family members responding to dysfunction by becoming emotionally distant and running away.

2. *Sabotage:* When employees feel unable to express their feelings and opinions, they sometimes resort to acting them out by violating rules, sabotaging the company, and so on.

    Example: In a large company, an employee recently shared a confidential, sensitive memo with a friend who worked for a competitor. The memo became front-page headlines.

Present information.

7–15 minutes.

If time allows, ask for examples and encourage discussion.

3. *Substance abuse:* Employees feeling excessive stress at work may respond as they would in a family, by abusing substances at work or after hours.

4. *Overachieving:* Companies with very high expectations may create employees who routinely produce miracles. This may look admirable to an outsider, but it can produce burnout among the employees. This dynamic resembles the family that looks perfect from the outside but is in fact severely dysfunctional.

5. *Underachieving:* Employees who feel unappreciated or abused may respond by producing substandard results at work, just as such family members do at home.

   Example: Most stores today have sales associates who act as if the customer is an interruption. These employees appear to have no interest in the success of the company.

6. *Emotional or physical abuse:* In some organizations, employees are routinely subjected to emotional or even physical abuse. These are obviously examples of severe dysfunction, just as they are when they occur in a family.

   Example: There have recently been several reports of physical and emotional abuse in the military.

7. *Double bind:* Some work teams have an atmosphere where employees feel "damned if you do and damned if you don't."

V.
Strategies for Resolving Problems

Following an assessment, the following family therapy interventions may help the employees of a dysfunctional company relate with one another in a healthier and more productive way.

(Note to discussion leader: Ask for examples of each of these interventions. Prepare a few examples of your own to illustrate some of these points as well.)

1. Teach employees the following communication and problem-solving skills:

   - How to define problems in a nonblaming way
   - How to listen with empathy
   - How to make requests assertively
   - How to brainstorm solutions

2. Help employees identify themes and company (family) myths. Explore those that may be discussed and challenged, as well as those that may not.

Activity column:

Present information.

10–15 minutes.

If time allows, ask for examples and encourage discussion.

3. Triangulation is the process whereby two people side against a third. Teach employees to manage conflict by teaching them how to avoid triangulation.

4. Where a work team shows signs of being disengaged, help employees build stronger relationships and communication patterns. Use team-building techniques to accomplish this.

5. Where the system is enmeshed, help the employees strengthen boundaries and increase autonomy. Team-building exercises can be helpful here, too.

6. Teach supervisors how to manage employees more effectively through regular supervisory skills training. Just as parents benefit from parenting skills training, supervisors need similar instruction.

Supervisory training should address the following skills:

- How to demonstrate effective listening skills
- How to encourage open communication among team members
- How to empower team members by setting effective goals
- How to encourage creativity and initiative
- How to resolve conflict in a healthy and productive manner

The goal of such interventions is to energize employees by teaching them new ways to relate to one another.

VI.
What to Do If the Boss Is the "Problem Patient"

The positive effects of any organizational intervention will be restricted by a lack of commitment and support from the boss. However, employees can encourage behavior change or "manage upward" in the following ways:

1. Communicate with the boss assertively rather than aggressively or passively.

2. Reward the boss for desired behaviors. For example, when the boss agrees to implement a change or request, positively reinforce the behavior by saying, "Thank you for allowing us to make this change."

3. Teach employees to focus on managing their own reactions to the boss's undesirable behavior. For example, teach them coping skills such as the following:

- Assertiveness skills
- Communication skills
- Negotiation skills

Present information.

7–15 minutes.

If time allows, ask for examples and encourage discussion.

You may wish to incorporate information from other workshop outlines, such as "Increasing Emotional Intelligence in the Workplace" and "How to Create a Positive Work Environment."

- Conflict resolution skills
- Relaxation skills

4. Encourage employees to be gently persistent in asking for what they want and stating the reasons it is important.

5. Team up with other departments and gather support for the change you seek.

6. Encourage employee participation by creating a suggestion box. Have a process for reviewing and talking about the suggestions.

VII. Conclusion

I hope you have enjoyed today's workshop. In the time remaining, I would be happy to answer any questions you may have.

Conclude the workshop.

Handout 8.1 Does Your Company Need Family Therapy?

1. How companies are like families:

   _____

   _____

2. Four dynamics that we bring to work from home:

   • _____

   • _____

   • _____

   • _____

3. Seven signs that the work/family relationship may be dysfunctional:

   • _____

   • _____

   • _____

   • _____

   • _____

   • _____

   • _____

4. Six strategies for resolving the work group's problems:

   • _____

   • _____

   • _____

   • _____

   • _____

   • _____

5. What to do if the boss is the "problem patient":

   • _____

   • _____

   • _____

   • _____

   • _____

   • _____

Chapter 9

Take Charge of Your Life:
Plan Your Best Year Yet!

Presentation Synopsis

In this workshop, participants explore the art and science of setting goals that motivate and inspire; they learn how achievements are produced and how to achieve more, ways to work more effectively and productively, how to make better use of time, and how to remove the obstacles to achieving outstanding results in life. The workshop is a combination of lecture, written exercises, and group discussion.

This presentation refers to information from the following book. You may wish to review it as you prepare your presentation.

Richardson, Cheryl. *Take Time for Your Life*. New York: Broadway Books, 1998.

Time Requirements

This presentation runs from 1½ to 2 hours, depending on the style of the presenter and the number of interactive activities used.

⏱ **Clock symbol.** This means that the information is included for a longer seminar or workshop. Omit these sections for a shorter presentation. If time is limited, another way to shorten your presentation is to share the information in lecture format. However, keep in mind that it is often harder to engage and maintain the audience's interest with pure lecture style. Unless you are a particularly dynamic speaker, you will probably want to keep at least a few of the exercises to enliven the presentation.

How to Use This Presentation

Possible Audiences	Whom to Contact
Businesspeople	Company presidents, human resources managers or other executives; Chamber of Commerce, Rotary, and similar business groups
PTO/PTA	PTO/PTA president
Women's civic and professional organizations	Director of educational programs
Adult education groups at churches and synagogues	Director of adult education programs

Sample Text for Marketing Letter, Brochure, or Postcard

Would the members of your organization like to be more productive in the coming year? _____ is offering an educational and motivational seminar to your group as a community service.

In this workshop, participants explore the art and science of setting goals that motivate and inspire; they learn how achievements are produced and how to achieve more, ways to work more effectively and productively, how to make better use of time, and how to remove the obstacles to achieving outstanding results in life. The workshop is a combination of lecture, written exercises, and group discussion.

_____ is a licensed _____ in private practice in _____. S/he specializes in _____ and _____. Call _____ today to schedule your group's **free** workshop. (_____) _____-_____.

Sample Text for Press Release

_____ Presents "Take Charge of Your Life" Workshop

_____ is presenting a **free** workshop on how to create a life for yourself that reflects your personal values and life goals. The workshop is scheduled for _____, from _____ to at _____. The workshop is limited to _____ participants and is open to Chamber of Commerce members and the public.

"Most people never think about how great achievements are produced," said _____, who will lead the workshop. "Setting motivating and inspiring goals is actually part art and part science, and there are some very specific steps that one should follow. This workshop helps participants achieve more, work more productively, make better use of time, and remove the obstacles to achieving outstanding results in life."

_____ is a licensed _____ in private practice in _____. S/he specializes in _____ and _____. For reservations, call _____ at (_____) _____-_____.

Exhibit 9.1 Presentation Outline

Take Charge of Your Life: Plan Your Best Year Yet!

Topic	*Time Estimate*
I. Introduction	
A. Introduce yourself	1 minute
B. Ask group members to introduce themselves	10 minutes
C. State workshop goals	1 minute
II. Why have goals?	2–4 minutes
III. Characteristics of effective goals	15 minutes
IV. Achievement process	10–15 minutes
V. Keys to effectiveness	3 minutes
VI. 80/20 rule	4–5 minutes
VII. High-payoff planning	17 minutes
VIII. Force-field analysis	11 minutes
IX. Seven common obstacles	10 minutes
X. Your action plan	5 minutes
XI. Conclusion	1 minute
Approximate total time	**90–98 minutes**

Exhibit 9.2 Presentation Script

Take Charge of Your Life: Plan Your Best Year Yet!

Outline	Presenter's Comments	Activity
I-A. **Introduce** **Yourself**	My name is _____. I'm a licensed _____, with a _____. I specialize in working with _____, and became interested in helping people achieve their goals when _____ _____.	Refer to your bio on the first page of the handouts. 1 minute.
I-B. **Group Intro** 🕐	I'd like to begin today's workshop by finding out a bit about each of you. Let's go around the room, introduce yourself, and tell us one thing you would like to accomplish in the coming year.	If the group is under 20 people, ask participants to introduce themselves. 10 minutes.
I-C. **Workshop** **Goals**	The purpose of today's workshop is to help you get started developing goals and an action plan that will make this your best year yet.	State goals. 1 minute.
II. **Why Have** **Goals?** 🕐	You may take notes beginning with Handout 9.1. Why is it important to have goals? Goals keep people healthy and sane. Without goals, people become less healthy, both mentally and physically. Can you think of some examples of this fact? **Types of answers to look for:** • People who die soon after they retire • People who are widowed who die soon after their mates die • The feeling of letdown after graduation from school or completing a major project You can have goals for all areas of your life, not just for work. The list on Handout 9.1 gives you some ideas for areas where you may want to set goals.	Handout 9.1. Lead discussion; list responses on blank easel. 2 minutes. When listing is complete, write HEALTH across the easel. Lead discussion. 2 minutes. If time is limited, present information as a lecture.
III. **Characteristics** **of Effective** **Goals**	Not all goals are motivating. If a goal is too vague, hard to measure, or impossible to achieve, it will lack effectiveness and ultimately be a wasted exercise. Handout 9.2 lists the characteristics of an effective goal.	Handout 9.2. Present information. 2 minutes.

9.5

Outline	Presenter's Comments	Activity

In addition to being written down, goal statements should:

- Be stated with action verbs
- Be Specific
- Be measurable
- Be challenging
- Include completion dates

Effective goals have all five ingredients. Let's discuss the five ingredients and examples of each that you will find on Handout 9.2.

Handout 9.2.

Please complete the practice exercise on Handout 9.3. Give yourself about five minutes. When you are finished, we'll discuss your answers.

Handout 9.3.
5 minutes.

Sample answers:

Discuss answers.
8 minutes.

1. Get my substitute teaching credential.

   - What element is missing from this goal? *Completion date.*
   - How could it be rewritten to make it more effective? *Get my substitute teaching credential by October 1.*

2. Get my house ready to sell by June 1.

   - What element is missing from this goal? *Specific, measurable.*
   - How could it be rewritten to make it more effective? *By June 1, have my house painted inside and out, replace the front door, and wash all windows.*

3. Get a job by May 15.

   - What element is missing from this goal? *Specific.*
   - How could it be rewritten to make it more effective? *Get a job as a department manager at Marshall Fields, Bloomingdale's, Sears, JCPenney, or Neiman-Marcus by May 15.*

IV. Achievement Process

Now that you know how to write effective goals, let's talk about another important subject: how goals are accomplished. The process of achieving anything includes three phases. These are detailed on Handout 9.4.

Handout 9.4.
Present information.
10 minutes.

1. *Ideas:* Choices or options. Having options tends to make us feel uncomfortable. In fact, having too many choices makes some people feel confused, frustrated, or even a bit crazy.

Ideas can seem like they actually have mass. People sometimes feel burdened with too many thoughts and ideas, and then feel lightened up when they move on to the next stage of the Achievement Process.

2. *Activity:* Doing something about the idea. Taking action. Getting started.

3. *Achievement:* When the idea takes on physical form—the report is written, the living room is painted, and so on.

You can feel satisfied or complete at any point in this cycle. Feeling satisfied results in:

- Energy
- Satisfaction
- Pleasure
- Power

. . . and you decide what completion is.

For example: Stella sewed a dress for a special occasion. She worked on it for several days. She had problems putting the zipper in the dress and never quite got it right. Every time someone compliments her on the beautiful dress, she has a hard time accepting the compliment and feels a knot in her stomach.

Just knowing where you are in the Achievement Process can help you feel complete. This can mean deciding, "I'm going to redo the zipper next Saturday," or "I'm going to shop for paint tomorrow," and so on.

The rate at which you move through the Achievement Process determines your sense of power. Anything you do to move something further along the process increases your sense of power.

If time allows, ask for more examples.

5 minutes.

I'd like to hear your examples of how the Achievement Process has operated in your life.

V. Keys to Effectiveness

1. Know what stage you are in with a given project. Get thoughts out of your head and onto a list.

Present information.

3 minutes.

2. Learn to be effective in all three stages of the Achievement Process. Learn where you specialize in the process, and strengthen the two places where you are less capable. You can compensate for your weaker areas by surrounding yourself with people who do specialize in those areas. You will be more effective as a team.

Outline	Presenter's Comments	Activity
	Handout 9.5 introduces some useful information that will help you do *high-payoff planning*.	Handout 9.5.
	Would you rather be effective or efficient? Management theorist Peter Drucker says that:	
	• Efficiency is doing a thing right. • Effectiveness is doing the right thing.	
VI. **80/20 Rule**	The 80/20 rule (also known as the Pareto Principle) says that 20 percent of what we do produces 80 percent of the results.	Present information. 3 minutes.
	Here are a few examples:	
	• 20 percent of the area in your house requires 80 percent of the cleaning. • 20 percent of the stocks in an investor's portfolio produce 80 percent of the results. • 20 percent of the kids in a class cause 80 percent of the problems. • 20 percent of the books in a bookstore account for 80 percent of the sales.	
	Who can think of other examples?	Ask for examples.
	Why is this important? What does it have to do with goals?	1 minute. Lead discussion.
	Answer to look for: It's important to remind yourself not to get bogged down in low-value activities, but to stay focused on the high-value 20 percent.	1 minute.
VII. **High-Payoff Planning**	Handout 9.6 defines high- and low-payoff activities and outlines several strategies for dealing with them:	Handout 9.6. Present information. 5 minutes. Ask for examples. Encourage discussion as time allows.
	High-payoff (HIPO) time is the 20 percent that produces the desired results. There are a few examples listed on the handout. What others can you think of?	
	Low-payoff (LOPO) time is the 80 percent that produces only 20 percent of the results. There are a few examples listed on the handout. What others can you think of?	
	The challenge is to find the HIPO tasks and *work on those first*.	
	The HIPO strategies:	Present information.
	• Setting a deadline increases the chances that you will accomplish a task.	

Outline	Presenter's Comments	Activity

- Setting a specific time to do something increases the chances that you will accomplish it.
- Divide and conquer: Break a task into smaller pieces and it becomes easier to complete.
- Motivate yourself by listing the benefits of completing a task.
- Motivate yourself in another way by rewarding yourself for completing a task.

The LOPO strategies:

- Dump: Don't do it at all.
- Delay: Do it later.
- Do it with minimum time investment or at a lower standard.

Handout 9.7 provides the next exercise. Think of your own life and list at least two high-payoff and two low-payoff targets and the activities that contribute directly toward each.

Handout 9.7.
Complete exercise.
3 minutes.

Take about two or three minutes. When the time is up, I'd like to ask two or three people to share what they wrote.

Lead discussion.
3 minutes.

Now that you have identified both high- and low-payoff items, take a moment to concentrate on the low-payoff tasks. Handout 9.8 is a worksheet that will help you zero in on these items and design an action plan to eliminate their influence.

Handout 9.8.
Complete exercise.
3 minutes.

Take a few minutes to work on this. When you're finished, I'll ask a few of you to share what you wrote.

Lead discussion.
3 minutes.

I want to encourage you to continue working on this exercise after the workshop. Identifying and writing these items down increases the chances that they will be accomplished.

VIII. Force-Field Analysis

For every goal that you set, there are conditions (forces) that *encourage* its completion. There are also conditions that *discourage* its completion.

Handout 9.9.
Present information.
5 minutes.

Handout 9.9 will help you identify two kinds of forces:

1. The forces that are pushing *with* you as you work toward your goal (encouraging forces)
2. The forces that are pushing *against* you (discouraging forces)

The process of force-field analysis (developed by scientist Kurt Lewin) is based on a law of physics that says that when

Outline	Presenter's Comments	Activity

two equal but opposite forces push against one another, there is no movement.

Why is this important to a person working toward a goal?

Answer to look for:

Because a similar dynamic can prevent you from achieving your goal.

The idea here is to *avoid paralysis* and encourage momentum by increasing positive (encouraging) forces and decreasing negative (discouraging) forces.

For example:

Goal: Get promoted to director level in the year 2XXX.

Discouraging forces:

- A possible merger with another company may result in excess talent at my level.
- I don't have an MBA.
- I sometimes convey a lack of self-confidence.

Encouraging forces:

- I have completed three major projects during the past year that have given me recognition.
- I have been with the company for five years.
- My last overall performance appraisal rating was outstanding.

After identifying as many encouraging and discouraging forces as possible, you can map a strategy to build on your strengths—the forces in your favor—and reduce the barriers.

Choose a goal of your own and make a list of the encouraging and discouraging forces. Take about three minutes, and then I'll ask a few of you to share what you wrote.

IX. Seven Obstacles

In *Take Time for Your Life,* author Cheryl Richardson lists seven obstacles that often block people from living the kind of life they desire. You may wish to write these down on Handout 9.10. For each, think about how it is true in your life.

The seven obstacles are:

1. *You think* selfish *is a dirty word.* Richardson says that many people have a difficult time putting their needs

Activity column:

Lead discussion.

Present information.

Individual exercise.

3 minutes.

Group discussion.

3 minutes.

Handout 9.10.

Present information.

7 minutes.

before others. As a result, they may feel frustrated and resentful because they are spending time on things they don't really want to do.

2. *Your schedule does not reflect your priorities.* Richardson says that this results in feeling exhausted at the end of the day without having accomplished what you want to do.

3. *You feel drained by people, places, and things.* You always have too much to do and it is not energizing.

4. *You feel trapped by money.* You think you can't make the choices you want because you don't have enough money to accomplish it.

5. *Your main source of fuel is adrenaline.* You are constantly running from one thing to the next, with no time to slow down.

6. *You don't have a support system.* You feel disconnected from people.

7. *You have no time to nourish your spirit.* You would like to pursue relaxing activities and take care of yourself, but there never seems to be time.

Who would like to share how any of these obstacles are true for you?

Lead discussion.

3 minutes.

X.
Your Action
Plan

Once you have identified the forces that favor and discourage the achievement of your goal, it's time to make an action plan. List each of the forces (positive and negative) you have identified in the previous exercise and answer the questions on Handout 9.10.

Handout 9.11.

Present information.

5 minutes.

For example: (*Continue with the example developed previously, or create a new example of your own*):

Force: No MBA

Actions I can take:

1. Send for information for enrolling in MBA programs at three local universities.
2. Talk to boss about why I should be promoted despite no MBA.
3. Research correlation of MBA and success in senior positions.

Outline	Presenter's Comments	Activity
	Who can help me:	
	1. My friend Bob, who works in Human Resources 2. My friend Susan, who has mastered conducting research on the Internet 3. My friend Jenny, who is an expert negotiator	
XI. **Conclusion**	I want to wish you all a focused and productive year.	Conclude the workshop. 1 minute.

Handout 9.1   Goals

Reasons to have goals: _____

_____

_____

_____

_____

Goal areas:

Knowledge	Service	Home
Adventure	Contribution	Wardrobe
Fantasy	Family	Spiritual matters
Emotions	Career	Church
Hobbies	Travel	Politics
Interests	Finances	Community
Studies	Income	Clubs
Reading	Net worth	Relationships
Exploring	Health	Professional matters
Communication		

Handout 9.2   How to Write Goals That Motivate

Necessary Ingredient	Example
Use action verbs.	• *Paint* house. • *Reduce* weight. • *Enroll in* college classes.
Use specific language.	• Paint *all bedrooms.* • Reduce weight *to 130 pounds.* • Enroll in *English 201.*
Specify measurable outcomes.	• *Paint one bedroom each week in February, to be completed by February 28.* • *Reduce weight to 130 pounds by March 15.* • *Enroll in English 201 in the spring term at community college.*
Challenge yourself without being unreachable.	• *Paint one bedroom each week in February, to be completed by February 28,* **not** *paint two rooms each week in February, with the entire house to be completed by February 15.* • *Reduce weight to 130 pounds by March 15,* **not** *reduce weight by 20 pounds in one month.* • *Enroll in English 201 in the spring term at community college* **not** *enroll in five classes and audit two classes in the spring term at community college.*
Specify completion dates.	• Paint one bedroom each week in February, *to be completed by February 28.* • Reduce weight to 130 pounds *by March 15.* • Enroll in English 201 in the spring term at community college *by January 1.*

Handout 9.3   How to Write Effective Goals

The goals listed here lack at least one of the important qualities we just discussed. Please identify what is missing and rewrite each goal. As you are evaluating the goals, be sure to look for these elements:

- Is stated with action verbs
- Is specific
- Is measurable
- Presents a challenge
- Includes completion dates

1. Get my substitute teaching credential.

   - What element is missing from this goal? _____

   - How could it be rewritten to make it more effective?

   _____

2. Get my house ready to sell by June 1.

   - What element is missing from this goal? _____

   - How could it be rewritten to make it more effective?

   _____

3. Get a job by May 15.

   - What element is missing from this goal? _____

   - How could it be rewritten to make it more effective?

   _____

1.

_____

2.

_____

3.

_____

Keys to effectiveness:

1. _____

2. _____

Handout 9.5 High-Payoff Planning

Would you rather be effective or efficient?

- Efficiency _____

- Effectiveness _____

The 80/20 rule (Pareto Principle)

Definition _____

_____

Examples

- 20 percent of the _____ causes 80 percent of the _____

- 20 percent of the _____ produces 80 percent of the _____

20%

80%

Time

80%

20%

Result

20%

Hi-Po Strategies

- Set specific deadlines
- Set specific times
- Divide & conquer
- List the benefits
- Reward yourself

Health
Satisfaction
Money
Advancement
Extra time
Accomplishment
_____

_____

_____

80%

_____
_____
_____

Lo-Po Strategies

Dump, Delay, or Do with minimum time investment

Handout 9.7   Identify Your High-Payoff Targets

What are your high-payoff targets?

List your high-payoff activities that contribute directly toward those targets.

Personal Life

1. Target: _____
   a. _____
   b. _____
   c. _____
   d. _____

2. Target: _____
   a. _____
   b. _____
   c. _____
   d. _____

3. Target: _____
   a. _____
   b. _____
   c. _____
   d. _____

Professional Life

4. Target: _____
   a. _____
   b. _____
   c. _____
   d. _____

5. Target: _____
   a. _____
   b. _____
   c. _____
   d. _____

6. Target: _____
   a. _____
   b. _____
   c. _____
   d. _____

Handout 9.8   Minimize Low-Payoff Tasks

List low-payoff items:

What can you do to spend less time on these items?

1. _____

    a. _____

    b. _____

    c. _____

    d. _____

2. _____

    a. _____

    b. _____

    c. _____

    d. _____

3. _____

    a. _____

    b. _____

    c. _____

    d. _____

4. _____

    a. _____

    b. _____

    c. _____

    d. _____

5. _____

    a. _____

    b. _____

    c. _____

    d. _____

6. _____

    a. _____

    b. _____

    c. _____

    d. _____

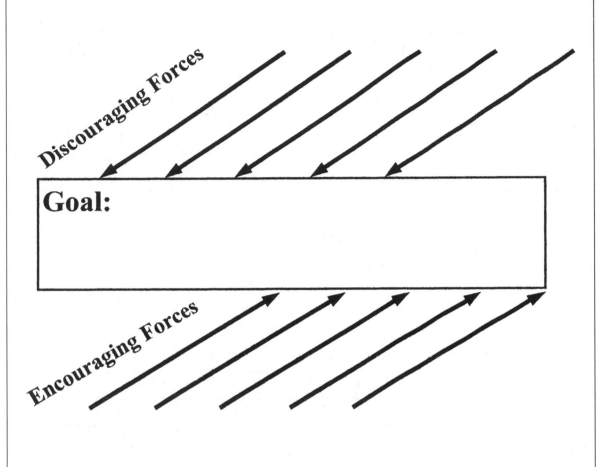

Goal:

Handout 9.10   Seven Common Obstacles

1. _____

   How this is true for me: _____

   _____

2. _____

   How this is true for me: _____

   _____

3. _____

   How this is true for me: _____

   _____

4. _____

   How this is true for me: _____

   _____

5. _____

   How this is true for me: _____

   _____

6. _____

   How this is true for me: _____

   _____

7. _____

   How this is true for me: _____

   _____

Handout 9.11   Your Action Plan

Force: _____

Actions you can take	Who can help you	Deadline
1. _____	1. _____	1. _____
2. _____	2. _____	2. _____
3. _____	3. _____	3. _____
4. _____	4. _____	4. _____

Force: _____

Actions you can take	Who can help you	Deadline
1. _____	1. _____	1. _____
2. _____	2. _____	2. _____
3. _____	3. _____	3. _____
4. _____	4. _____	4. _____

Force: _____

Actions you can take	Who can help you	Deadline
1. _____	1. _____	1. _____
2. _____	2. _____	2. _____
3. _____	3. _____	3. _____
4. _____	4. _____	4. _____

Force: _____

Actions you can take	Who can help you	Deadline
1. _____	1. _____	1. _____
2. _____	2. _____	2. _____
3. _____	3. _____	3. _____
4. _____	4. _____	4. _____

Chapter 10

Manage Your Stress

Presentation Synopsis

Through written exercises and group discussion, participants learn what stress is, how to measure it, what causes stress in the workplace, reasons that stress is harmful, how stress is worse today, what stresses are unique to women, how to protect yourself against stress, and how to develop a personal stress management plan.

This presentation refers to information from the following books. I recommend that you review them as you prepare your presentation.

Cunningham, J. Barton. *The Stress Management Sourcebook.* Los Angeles: Lowell House, 1997.

Davidson, Jeff. *The Complete Idiot's Guide to Managing Stress.* New York: Alpha Books, 1997.

Hanson, Peter G. *The Joy of Stress.* Kansas City, MO: Andrews & McMeel, 1985.

Hanson, Peter G. *Stress for Success.* New York: Doubleday, 1989.

Prevention's Guide to Stress-Free Living. Emmaus, PA: Rodale Press, 1998.

Viscott, David. *The Viscott Method.* New York: Pocket Books, 1984.

Time Requirements

This presentation runs from 1½ hours to 2 hours, depending on the style of the presenter and the number of interactive activities used.

⏲ **Clock symbol.** This means that the information is included for a longer seminar or workshop. Omit these sections for a shorter presentation. If time is limited, another way to shorten your presentation is to share the information in lecture format. However, keep in mind that it is often harder to engage and maintain the audience's interest with pure lecture style. Unless you are a particularly dynamic speaker, you will probably want to keep at least a few of the exercises to enliven the presentation.

Video examples. Showing selected scenes from popular movies is one way to make your presentation more interesting. It creates some variety and interest, stimulates discussion, and might be a way to inject some humor. Consider selecting short scenes from videos such as *Moscow on the Hudson, Broadcast News,* and *Lost in America.* Suggestions for specific scenes are included in this outline, but you are encouraged to look for other examples on your own as you prepare for your presentation. You may also wish to play theme music such as "Pressure" (by Billy Joel) as people enter the meeting room. If you plan to include scenes from videos, have the playback equipment set up and test it before you begin your presentation.

How to Use This Presentation

Possible Audiences	Whom to Contact
Adult education groups at churches and synagogues	Director of adult education programs
PTO/PTA	PTO/PTA president
Women's civic and professional organizations	Director of educational programs
Businesspeople	Company presidents, human resources managers, or other executives; Chamber of Commerce, Rotary, and similar business groups

Sample Text for Marketing Letter, Brochure, or Postcard

_____ is offering an educational and motivational seminar to your group as a community service. In this workshop, participants learn what stress is, how to measure it, what causes stress in the workplace, reasons that stress is harmful, how stress is worse today, what stresses are unique to women, how to protect yourself against stress, and how to develop a personal stress management plan.
_____ is a licensed _____ in private practice in _____.
S/he specializes in _____ and _____. Call _____ today to schedule your group's **free** workshop. (_____) _____-_____.

Sample Text for Press Release

_____ Presents "Manage Your Stress" Workshop

_____ is presenting a **free** workshop on how to manage stress at work and in your personal life. The workshop is scheduled for _____, from _____ to _____ at _____. The workshop is limited to ____ participants and is open to the public.
   According to _____, "Most people know that stress is harmful, but they may not know how to manage it. This workshop helps people develop a personal management plan that will help them protect against stress."
   _____ is a licensed _____ in private practice in _____.
S/he specializes in _____ and _____. For reservations, call _____ at (_____) _____-_____.

Exhibit 10.1   Presentation Outline

Manage Your Stress

Topic	Time Estimate
I. **Introduction**	
A. Introduce yourself	1 minute
🕐 B. Ask group members to introduce themselves	10 minutes
C. State workshop goals	1 minute
II. **What is stress?**	8 minutes
III. **How to measure stress**	18 minutes
IV. **Increased expectations**	5–7 minutes
🕐 Video example	
V. **Stress at work**	3–4 minutes
🕐 Video example	
VI. **Why is stress bad?**	3 minutes
VII. **Life without stress?**	3–4 minutes
🕐 Video example	
VIII. **How is stress worse today?**	3 minutes
IX. **Stresses unique to women**	3 minutes
X. **Protect yourself against stress**	39–41 minutes
🕐 A. Recognize how stress affects you	
B. Manage stress at work	
C. Workplace strategies	
D. Learn to have healthy relationships	
E. Diet	
F. Exercise	
G. Meditate and relax	
XI. **Relaxation exercise**	3 minutes
XII. **Your personal stress management plan**	11 minutes
XIII. **Conclusion**	
Approximate total time	**100–117 minutes**

10.4

Exhibit 10.2   Presentation Script

Manage Your Stress

Outline	Presenter's Comments	Activity
I-A. **Introduce** **Yourself**	My name is _____. I'm a licensed _____, with a _____. I specialize in working with _____, and became interested in helping my clients deal with stress about ____ ago, when I noticed that _____ _____.	Refer to your bio on the first page of the handouts. 1 minute.
I-B. **Group Intro**	I'd like to begin today's workshop by finding out something about each of you. Let's go around the room and each of you tell us your name and what brings you to this workshop.	If the group is under 20 people, ask participants to introduce themselves. 10 minutes.
I-C. **Goals**	In this workshop, we will explore what stress is and how to measure it. You will learn how to protect yourself against stress and, when you leave today, you will have begun to develop your own personal stress management plan.	State goals. 1 minute.
II. **What Is** **Stress?**	What is your definition of stress? You may want to take notes on Handout 10.1. Let's compare your ideas to what the experts say. Most experts define stress as a *response* to life situations like the following: • Being overloaded with responsibilities • Role ambiguity • Having to do unpleasant tasks • Too many distractions • Having to do tasks for which one is unprepared • Working with difficult people • Being bored • Being sick • Too many changes • Physical danger • Living or working in a crowded space • Not getting enough exercise • Poor nutrition • Not getting enough sleep • Not enough downtime	Lead discussion. Handout 10.1. List responses on blank easel. 5 minutes.

Outline	Presenter's Comments	Activity
	• Being dissatisfied with your physical appearance • Drug and alcohol abuse	
	Now take a minute to answer the question at the bottom of Handout 10.1.	Individual exercise.
	When you are finished, I'd like to ask two or three participants to share what you identified as your most significant sources of stress.	Lead group discussion. 3 minutes.
III. **How to** **Measure** **Stress**	In 1967, Thomas Holmes and Richard Rahe (of the University of Washington) developed a list of 42 common stress-producing experiences, which included changes in family, job, personal relationships, and so on. Handout 10.2 is an adaptation of the scale they developed. It was originally known as the Holmes-Rahe Scale. It can be found in many of today's books on managing stress.	Present information. Handout 10.2. 5 minutes.
	Take about five minutes to complete the scale. When you are finished, we will discuss how to interpret the scores.	
	According to J. Barton Cunningham in *The Stress Management Sourcebook,* this is how to interpret scores on the Life Events Scale:	Present information. 3 minutes.
	A high score does *not* mean that a person will inevitably become ill. The test is just a guideline and can help you understand your life situation and make a plan for managing stressful times.	
	150 to 199 indicates mild life change or possibility to be stressed. Holmes and Rahe indicated that 37 percent of the people who scored in this range had an appreciable change in their health.	
	200 to 299 indicates moderate life change. People in this category have a fifty-fifty chance of experiencing a change in their health.	
	Over 300 indicates a major life change. Seventy percent of the people studied by Holmes and Rahe who scored above 300 had some illness in the following year.	
	I'd like to ask a few of you to comment on what you noticed when you completed this questionnaire.	Lead discussion. 10 minutes.
	• What surprised you? • What concerns you? • What makes sense?	

Outline	Presenter's Comments	Activity

Notice that the scale includes both pleasant and unpleasant events. Both can be stressful. What comments do you have about that?

Why is it important to consider individual responses to stressful events?

Answer to look for:

People have unique perceptions of what is stressful and what is not. These perceptions play a huge role in who is affected by stress and who is less affected.

IV. Increased Expectations

Stress has become a lifestyle in our culture in the last 20 years for reasons other than the events that happen to each of us. Think about how our expectations of speed and efficiency have risen so dramatically.

Present information.

2 minutes.

What impact have things like ATM machines, microwave ovens, and fax machines had on all of us?

Lead discussion.

Answer to look for:

These phenomena have made life more convenient in many ways, but they also have woven an expectation of instant gratification into our culture. And this causes stress.

Video Example

In the movie *Moscow on the Hudson,* Robin Williams plays a Russian immigrant. This is how his character responds to being overwhelmed with the many choices we all face on a typical trip to the grocery store. *(Show the scene where Robin Williams faints in the grocery store when faced with too many kinds of coffee to buy.)*

What are other examples of products and services that were invented to make life more efficient and productive, but which sometimes seem instead to add to stress because they have raised expectations that life can move faster than ever?

2 minutes.

Answers to look for:

- 24-hour stores and restaurants
- 1-hour photo developing
- Drive-thru fast food
- 10-minute oil change
- Web sites providing instant access to unlimited information

Lead discussion.

3 minutes.

Outline	Presenter's Comments	Activity
	• Catalog and Internet shopping • Personal computers • E-mail • *CNN Headline News* • 30-minute pizza delivery	
V. **Stress at** **Work**	Stress affects people in every type of work setting. • *People at the top* of organizations suffer from stress because of excessive workloads, unrealistic expectations, and isolation. The phrase "it's lonely at the top" has some truth to it. • *Middle managers* often experience stress because they have responsibility for the people who report to them but lack the control to execute what is expected. With the recent epidemic of corporate downsizing, middle managers have also been given greater and greater workloads. Managers who manage to keep their jobs often feel like they are living in the shadow of termination. • *Professionals* suffer from their own brand of stress caused by monotony. Doctors, lawyers, and other professionals often perform the same kind of work for many years, resulting in boredom and desperation. • Workers at the *lower levels* of today's organizations often feel stress caused by boredom and the frustration of dealing with the public. They also may feel less successful than their coworkers in higher-level jobs and may feel stressed by their lack of status.	Present information. 3 minutes.
⏱ **Video** **Example**	(*Show the scene from* Five Easy Pieces *with Jack Nicholson and the waitress.*)	Show video. 1 minute.
VI. **Why Is Stress** **Bad?**	Why do you think stress is a bad thing? **Answers to look for:** According to *The Stress Management Sourcebook,* stress causes the following kinds of diseases (page 34): • Cardiovascular system diseases. (One heart attack occurs in the United States every 32 seconds.) • Digestive system diseases. (Ulcers affect 10 percent of us.)	Lead discussion. 3 minutes. Note responses on the flip chart.

Outline	Presenter's Comments	Activity

- Immune system diseases. (300,000 people die of cancer each year in North America.)
- Musculoskeletal system disease. (American workers lose 200 million workdays each year because of rheumatoid arthritis.)
- Emotional and psychological disorders. (These manifest in emotional disturbances, alcohol and drug abuse, or divorce.)

VII.
Life without Stress?

I'd like to show you a scene from the movie *Lost in America,* where, having left his high-stress life in Los Angeles, Albert Brooks is working as a school crossing guard. He is miserable and spends the rest of the film working toward getting his old life back.

Show video.
1 minute.

Video Example

Brooks's character impulsively left his job as an advertising executive climbing the corporate ladder in Los Angeles. He thought he would love the stress-free life of a crossing guard, but he never enjoyed it for a minute. How could a life of no stress turn out to be so stressful?

Lead discussion.
3 minutes.

Possible answer:

Brooks went from being overstimulated to being understimulated. Boredom can be very stressful. He also had financial stresses, which the crossing guard job only compounded.

VIII.
How Is Stress Worse Today?

Why do you think stress has become more of a problem in recent years?

Lead discussion.
3 minutes.

Answers to look for:

1. The nature of work has changed. The fight-or-flight responses to stress are ineffective in response to the stresses of today's life.

2. The workplace has become decentralized. People no longer work together in one place, but may be scattered around the world and connected by technology.

3. People change with each generation. Baby Boomers differ from Generation Xers in terms of their values, their work ethic, and their definitions of success. These generational differences contribute to stress at work.

Outline	Presenter's Comments	Activity
IX. **Stresses** **Unique to** **Women**	What stress problems are unique to women?	Lead discussion. 3 minutes.

Answers to look for:

1. Women are still paid less than men for the same work.
2. Women still face a "glass ceiling" as they climb the corporate ladder. Only 2 percent of the members of top management of North American corporations are women.
3. Women who choose to have children are usually responsible for the logistics of child care.
4. Women often do more housework when they get home than their husbands do.
5. Women with children also tend to experience guilt feelings about leaving their children to go to work.

Outline	Presenter's Comments	Activity
X. **Protect** **Yourself** **against Stress**	In *The Stress Management Sourcebook,* author Cunningham outlines the following six principles for managing stress. These are outlined on Handout 10.3.	Present information. 15 minutes. Handout 10.3.

1. Recognize how stress affects you.
2. Manage stress at work.
3. Learn to have healthy relationships.
4. Watch your diet.
5. Exercise.
6. Meditate and relax.

Let's look at each of these strategies.

Outline	Presenter's Comments	Activity
X-A. **Recognize** **How Stress** **Affects You**	Each of us responds differently to a given stressful situation. An important part of learning to manage stress is to know yourself and understand what makes you feel stressed.	Lead discussion. 2 minutes.

A well-publicized study of how personality is related to stress introduced the concept of the Type A personality. The study was outlined in a book called *Type A Behavior and Your Heart.* The authors, Meyer Friedman and Ray Rosenman, studied 80 people who were identified as having Type A personalities. They compared these people with a control group with Type B personality characteristics. The two personality types were described as follows:

Type A	**Type B**
• Competitive	• Relaxed
• Aggressive	• Takes time to enjoy life
• Works fast	• Has enough time

Type A   **Type B**

- Impatient   - Moves and speaks slowly
- Restless   - Not a social climber
- Feels time urgency   - Works steadily

The researchers found that people with Type A personality characteristics had a rate of coronary heart disease that was *seven times higher* than that of the control group.

People with more Type B personality characteristics have a much smaller incidence of heart disease. Let's talk about how you can develop more Type B personality characteristics.

- Make the commitment to cultivate Type B characteristics.
- Recognize the benefits of Type B.
- Recognize the dangers of Type A.
- Schedule fewer tasks.
- Take on fewer, not more, commitments.
- Learn and practice relaxation techniques.
- Manage your time better.
- Explore your feelings of dissatisfaction with your achievements.
- Ask yourself why you expect so much of yourself.
- Learn ways to manage anger productively.
- Practice cognitive therapy techniques for changing nonproductive thoughts.
- Evaluate your self-esteem and look for ways to build it.
- Identify perfectionist tendencies and self-blame; work on accepting yourself and your limitations.

What other ideas would you add?

X-B. Manage Stress at Work

Many work environments encourage us to act like Type A people. Even if the behaviors that are considered Type A are not your natural style, you may find yourself leaning in that direction if you work in an organization that is:

Present information.

10 minutes.

- Competitive
- Perfectionistic
- Fast-moving
- Poorly organized
- In conflict
- Highly political

Stress at work most often results from the following:

- Too much or too little work
- Work that is very complicated and demanding
- Work that is boring and repetitive
- Unclear goals and expectations
- Changing or confusing procedures
- A career dead end
- An impersonal management philosophy

X-C.
Workplace
Strategies

What are some examples of each kind of stress (in preceding list)?

Activity: Lead discussion.

Here are three strategies for dealing with workplace stress:

Activity: Present information. 3 minutes.

1. Clarify your career goals. Are the trade-offs of working in a high-stress organization worth the benefits gained?

2. Assess your values and interests. Are your needs being met in your current organization? If not, would a change better meet your needs?

3. Identify the specific sources of stress in your organization. What changes are needed? Are you in a position to influence change in a positive direction? What would it take? Is it worth it?

X-D.
Learn to
Have Healthy
Relationships

"Learning to have healthy relationships" could be a training program several years long. In the short time we have together today, let's look at the key components of this stress-reducing strategy.

Activity: Present information. 5 minutes.

You may wish to take a few notes on Handout 10.3 in the spaces provided.

1. *Identify the sources of stress in your relationships.* Write about it in a journal. Make a list of people who cause you stress and explore what the issues are.

2. *Resolve the underlying issues.* For each of the situations identified in the preceding step, assess what needs to happen to resolve it. Make a list and design a plan to improve the situation.

3. *Learn skills to improve relationships.* Relationship skills are learned. We are not born knowing how to get along well with others, and most of us learned only limited skills from our parents. Identify the skills you need to develop and make a plan for yourself. Skills can be

learned by reading books, taking classes, or working with a therapist.

4. *Avoid people and situations where positive relationships are impossible.* Some people have a toxic effect on you. If possible, limit the amount of time you spend in these situations. Look for opportunities to decline their invitations.

   For work situations, look for ways to rearrange your schedule or your work space to avoid interacting with such people.

   When these people are family members, remind yourself that you don't have to feel guilty about avoiding anyone who makes you feel bad about yourself.

5. *Seek out positive people and situations.* This step is the reverse of the previous step. Look for opportunities to spend more time with people and in situations that make you feel good. Think about people who make you feel good about yourself and look for ways to increase time with them.

**X-E.
Watch Your
Diet**

Some foods exaggerate the stress response. These include the following:

Present
information.

2 minutes.

- *Caffeine* stimulates the release of stress hormones. This increases heart rate and blood pressure, and increases the amount of oxygen to the heart. Ongoing exposure to caffeine can harm the tissue of the heart.

- *Refined sugar* and processed flour are depleted of needed vitamins. In times of stress, certain vitamins help the body maintain the nervous and endocrine systems.

- Too much *salt* can lead to excessive fluid retention. This can lead to nervous tension and higher blood pressure. Stress often adds to the problem by causing increased blood pressure.

- *Smoking* not only causes disease and shortens life, it leads to increased heart rate, blood pressure, and respiration.

- *Alcohol* robs the body of nutrition that it might otherwise use for cell growth and repair. It also harms the liver and adds empty calories to the body.

During times of high stress, eat more complex carbo-hydrates (fruits, vegetables, whole breads, cereals, and beans).

Outline	Presenter's Comments	Activity
X-F. **Exercise**	The human body was designed to be physically active. However, in most jobs today, people are sitting down most of the time. They hardly move at all except when it is time for coffee break or lunch. When faced with stressors, we respond with our minds, not our bodies. It is no wonder that many of us have a difficult time responding to stressful events.	Present information. 3 minutes.
	Exercise is one of the simplest and most effective ways to respond to stress. Activity provides a natural release for the body during its fight-or-flight state of arousal. After exercising, the body returns to its normal state of equilibrium, and one feels relaxed and refreshed.	
	A recent issue of *The Prevention Guide to Stress-Free Living* suggested the following strategies to get yourself to exercise:	

1. Eat small meals every four hours to maintain a high energy level. Then you won't be too tired to exercise.

2. Work out late in the day instead of getting up at 4:30 A.M. to squeeze in a workout before work.

3. Focus on short-term, manageable exercise goals. You will be more likely to keep them.

4. Reward yourself at the end of each week when you stick to your goals.

5. Write in three exercise sessions each week on your calendar. Treat them like you would a business meeting and schedule your other activities around them.

6. Do paperwork while you walk on the treadmill or climb the stair climber. This may relieve boredom.

7. Keep a journal and track your results.

8. Exercise with a friend or lover. The companionship will make it more fun and lessen the chance that you will quit.

Outline	Presenter's Comments	Activity
X-G. **Meditate and** **Relax**	There are many ways to relax, refresh, and regenerate. Meditation and progressive relaxation are two valuable ways to let go of tension and anxiety. You can purchase audiotapes or record your own.	Present information. 1 minute.
	You will benefit most if you do meditation or relaxation exercises at the same time each day. Some people like to play a self-hypnosis tape when they get up in the morning,	

Outline	Presenter's Comments	Activity

and others do so when they get into bed at night. The important thing is to make the choice to take control of your own responses to stress.

XI. Relaxation Exercise

(You may choose to replace this exercise with one of your own. Consider playing a tape or CD of relaxing music in the background as you slowly read the following script.)

Take everything off your lap. Unfold your arms and uncross your legs, and place your hands on your knees. Allow your eyes to close. Take a deep breath as you listen to my voice.

Imagine yourself in a peaceful woods. You are facing a lake. Everywhere you look, you see comfort and tranquility. It is late afternoon. The light is soft and the air is still. You are looking across the glassy lake with the perfect reflection of a mountain on the other side. Place yourself in this scene and look about. Notice the details: You see wildflowers and tall trees, and you hear birds.

You are able to move great distances just by wishing. You picture yourself floating up to a mountain meadow at the edge of the timberline. You stand on the gentle slope. The air is clear and warm. The moment feels as free as an afternoon in your childhood. You look across the valley below at the pink and white clouds drifting by.

You notice a mossy path and follow it along a gurgling stream. You come to a pool with large boulders all around. You look into the pool and see your face reflected clearly. You look so serene. The more you look at your reflected face, the calmer you feel. Just ahead, you see the opening of a cave with an intense golden light coming from within. As you enter the cave, the light seems to pass through you, warming you and filling you with peace.

As you stand in this warm energy, you feel lighter. You feel yourself soaring free of all earthly bonds through the golden clouds. Away . . . free.

(Pause)

In a moment, bring yourself back into this room. Become aware of the chair you are sitting in and the sounds of the day. When you are ready, open your eyes.

(Note: this exercise is from The Viscott Method *[see Resource List], page 250.)*

Play relaxing background music.

Read relaxation script.

3 minutes.

Outline	Presenter's Comments	Activity
XII. **Your** **Personal** **Stress** **Management** **Plan**	Health and longevity depend on minimizing stress and achieving success and well-being. According to Peter Hanson, author of *The Joy of Stress,* any plan for managing stress and maximizing well-being should address four life areas (listed on Handout 10.4): 1. Personal relationships 2. Healthy lifestyle 3. Financial 4. Work life	Present information. Handout 10.4. 1 minute.
	Take a few moments to answer the questions on Handout 10.4. Allow five minutes. When you are finished, I'd like to have two or three of you discuss what you learned and what you plan to do as a result.	Complete exercise. 5 minutes. Lead group discussion. 5 minutes.
XIII. **Conclusion**	I hope you have enjoyed today's workshop. In the time remaining, I would be happy to answer any questions you may have.	Conclude the workshop.

Handout 10.1   Sources of Stress

Stress is a response to situations like these:

_____

_____

_____

_____

_____

_____

My five most stress-producing situations are:

1. _____

2. _____

3. _____

4. _____

5. _____

Handout 10.2   Life Events

For each of the events you have experienced in the past 12 months, give yourself the number of points indicated. If a given event happened more than once during this time period, multiply the points by the number of occurrences.

Life Event	Times It Happened	Value	Your Score
1. Death of a spouse	_____	100	_____
2. Divorce	_____	73	_____
3. Marital separation	_____	65	_____
4. Jail term	_____	63	_____
5. Death of a close family member	_____	63	_____
6. Personal injury or illness	_____	53	_____
7. Marriage	_____	50	_____
8. Fired at work	_____	47	_____
9. Marital reconciliation	_____	45	_____
10. Retirement	_____	45	_____
11. Change in health of a family member	_____	44	_____
12. Pregnancy	_____	40	_____
13. Sex difficulties	_____	39	_____
14. Gain of new family member	_____	39	_____
15. Business readjustment	_____	39	_____
16. Change in financial state	_____	38	_____
17. Death of a close friend	_____	37	_____
18. Change to a different line of work	_____	36	_____
19. Change in number of arguments with spouse	_____	35	_____
20. Mortgage over $150,000	_____	31	_____

Life Event	Times It Happened	Value	Your Score
21. Foreclosure of mortgage or loan	_____	30	_____
22. Change in responsibilities at work	_____	29	_____
23. Son or daughter leaving home	_____	29	_____
24. Trouble with in-laws	_____	29	_____
25. Outstanding personal achievement	_____	28	_____
26. Spouse begins or stops work	_____	26	_____
27. Begin or end school	_____	26	_____
28. Change in living conditions	_____	25	_____
29. Trouble with boss	_____	23	_____
30. Change in work hours or conditions	_____	23	_____
31. Change in residence	_____	20	_____
32. Change in schools	_____	20	_____
33. Change in recreation	_____	19	_____
34. Change in church activities	_____	19	_____
35. Change in social activities	_____	18	_____
36. Mortgage or loan less than $10,000	_____	17	_____
37. Change in sleeping habits	_____	16	_____
38. Change in number of family get-togethers	_____	15	_____
39. Change in eating habits	_____	15	_____
40. Vacation	_____	13	_____
41. Christmas	_____	12	_____
42. Minor violations of the law	_____	11	_____
Total Score	_____		_____

Source: Reprinted with permission from the *Journal of Psychosomatic Research,* vol. 11, pp. 213–218, by T. H. Holmes and R. H. Rahe, "The Social Readjustment Rating Scale," 1967, with permission of Elsevier Science.

Handout 10.3   Strategies for Managing Stress

1. Recognize how stress affects you.

   Type A characteristics: _____

   _____

   _____

   _____

   _____

   Type B characteristics: _____

   _____

   _____

   _____

   _____

   Ways to become less Type A and more Type B: _____

   _____

   _____

   _____

   _____

   _____

2. Manage stress at work. _____

   _____

   _____

   _____

   _____

3. Learn to have healthy relationships.

   - Identify the sources of stress in your relationships.

   - Resolve the underlying issues.

   - Learn skills to improve relationships.

   - Avoid people and situations where positive relationships are impossible.

   - Seek out positive people and situations.

4. Watch your diet.

- Caffeine

- Sugar

- Salt

- Smoking

- Alcohol

5. Exercise. _____

_____

_____

_____

_____

6. Meditate and relax. _____

_____

_____

_____

_____

Source: Adapted from *The Stress Management Sourcebook* by J. Barton Cunningham, PhD. Used with permission of NTC/Contemporary Publishing Group, Inc.

10.21

Handout 10.4   Manage Stress and Maximize Well-Being

Personal Relationships

Strengths: _____

_____

_____

_____

Areas needing improvement: _____

_____

_____

_____

Action plan: _____

_____

_____

_____

Healthy Lifestyle

Strengths: _____

_____

_____

_____

Areas needing improvement: _____

_____

_____

_____

Action plan: _____

_____

_____

_____

Financial Situation

Strengths: _____

_____

_____

_____

Areas needing improvement: _____

_____

_____

_____

Action plan: _____

_____

_____

_____

Work Life

Strengths: _____

_____

_____

_____

Areas needing improvement: _____

_____

_____

_____

Action plan: _____

_____

_____

_____

Adapted from Peter G. Hanson, MD, *The Joy of Stress* (Kansas City, MO: Andrews & McMeel, 1985), p. 193.

Chapter 11

How to Create a Positive Work Environment

Presentation Synopsis

In this workshop, participants learn specific ways to make the workplace more positive by motivating and reinforcing their coworkers. Skills are developed through lecture, group discussion, practice exercises, and analysis of popular movies.

This presentation contains information from the following books. I recommend that you review them as you prepare your presentation.

Nelson, Bob. *1001 Ways to Energize Employees.* New York: Workman, 1997.

Nelson, Bob. *1001 Ways to Reward Employees.* New York: Workman, 1994.

Time Requirements

This presentation runs from 1½ to 2 hours, depending on the style of the presenter and the number of interactive activities used.

🕐 **Clock symbol.** This means that the information is included for a longer seminar or workshop. Omit these sections for a shorter presentation. If time is limited, another way to shorten your presentation is to share the information in lecture format. However, keep in mind that it is often harder to engage and maintain the audience's interest with pure lecture style. Unless you are a particularly dynamic speaker, you will probably want to keep at least a few of the exercises to enliven the presentation.

Video examples. Showing selected scenes from popular movies is one way to make your presentation more interesting. It creates some variety and interest, stimulates discussion, and might be a way to inject some humor. Consider selecting short scenes from videos such as *Stand and Deliver, Dangerous Minds, The Dead Poets Society,* and *A League of Their Own.* Suggestions for specific scenes are included in this outline, but you are encouraged to look for other examples on your own as you prepare for your presentation.

How to Use This Presentation

Possible Audiences	**Whom to Contact**
Businesspeople	Company presidents, human resources managers, or other executives
Adult education groups at churches and synagogues	Director of adult education programs
Women's civic and professional organizations	Director of educational programs

Sample Text for Marketing Letter, Brochure, or Postcard

In today's challenging workplace, the ability to manage people is more important than ever. _____ is presenting a free workshop that will teach your managers specific ways to make your workplace more positive and motivating. Through lecture, group discussion, practice exercises, and analysis of popular movies, participants will learn dozens of ways to create a positive work environment that can lead to lower turnover and higher morale.

_____ is a licensed _____ in private practice in _____. S/he specializes in _____ and _____. Call _____ today to schedule your group's **free** workshop. (_____) _____-_____.

Sample Text for Press Release

_____ Presents Management Skills Workshop

_____ is presenting a **free** workshop on how to create a positive work environment. The workshop is scheduled for _____, from _____ to _____ at _____. The workshop is limited to ____ participants and is open to the public.

"We have all worked in places where we grew to dread getting up in the morning, and a few of us have had the pleasure of working for a boss who makes us feel like we can do anything," says _____. "Often negative work environments are the result of a lack of training. No one is born knowing how to manage others. These skills can be learned, starting with something as simple as this workshop."

_____ is a licensed _____ in private practice in _____. S/he specializes in _____ and _____. For reservations, call _____ at (_____) _____-_____.

Exhibit 11.1   Presentation Outline

How to Create a Positive Work Environment

Topic	*Time Estimate*
I. Introduction	
A. Introduce yourself	1 minute
B. Ask group members to introduce themselves	10 minutes
C. State workshop goals	1 minute
II. Positive versus negative work environment	7 minutes
Video example	2 minutes
III. Four key skills	
A. State your expectations	7 minutes
Video example	2 minutes
B. Show interest in your team	12 minutes
C. Create an encouraging environment	6 minutes
Video example	2 minutes
D. Recognize and reward good performance	15 minutes
IV. Reinforcement guidelines	10 minutes
V. Recognition guidelines	8 minutes
VI. Ideas for recognizing and rewarding good performance	20 minutes
VII. Conclusion	
Approximate total time	**87–103 minutes**

Exhibit 11.2   Presentation Script

How to Create a Positive Work Environment

Outline	Presenter's Comments	Activity
I-A. **Introduce** **Yourself**	My name is _____. I'm a licensed _____, with a _____. I specialize in working with _____, and became interested in helping people learn skills for managing others in the workplace when _____ _____.	Refer to your bio on the first page of the handouts. 1 minute.
I-B. **Group Intro** 🕐	I'd like to begin today's workshop by finding out a bit about each of you. Let's go around the room and each of you give your name and tell us something about yourself.	If the group is under 20 people, ask participants to introduce themselves. 10 minutes.
I-C. **Goals**	In this workshop, you will learn specific ways to make your workplace more positive by motivating and reinforcing your coworkers. The workshop will include some lecture, group discussion, practice exercises, and analysis of popular movies.	State goals. 1 minute.
II. **Positive** **versus** **Negative** **Workplaces**	We have all worked in places where we grew to dread getting up in the morning, and a few of us have had the pleasure of working for a boss who makes us feel like we can do anything. Let's begin by exploring the differences between a positive and a negative work environment.	Present information.
🕐 **Video** **Example**	You may remember the movie *A League of Their Own*. This is one of the most memorable scenes. *(Show the scene where Tom Hanks says, "There is no crying in baseball.")* How do you think Tom Hanks's team must have felt after he made this comment? What effect do you think this may have had on the team's motivation? I'd like a few of you to give us some examples of what it was like to work in a workplace where you felt bad versus one where you felt good. You may want to note these on Handout 11.1.	Show video. 1 minute. Lead discussion. 1 minute. Handout 11.1. List ideas on a blank easel pad. 5 minutes.

Outline	Presenter's Comments	Activity

Answers to look for:

Bad work environment:	Good work environment:
• Boss was unfriendly.	• Boss was interested in me.
• Boss was critical.	• Boss encouraged me.
• There was high turnover.	• Employees liked working there.
• There was low morale.	• There was company pride and loyalty.
• I watched the clock.	
• I never got any feedback.	• I knew where I stood.

Hundreds of books have been written on the subject of managing and motivating people. Hundreds of training seminars are conducted on this subject around the world every day. And yet it's interesting that even with all of this available information, few companies succeed at creating a positive work environment.

Present information.

2 minutes.

III.
Four Key Skills

Since our time together is limited today, we will focus on four of the most important skills that will help you create a positive work environment.

The four key skills are:

1. Tell people what you expect of them.
2. Show interest in your team members.
3. Create an encouraging environment.
4. Recognize and reward good performance.

III-A.
State Your Expectations

Let's look at the first skill, *tell people what you expect of them.* What does this mean to you?

Lead discussion.

2 minutes.

Answers to look for:

Telling people what you expect of them includes:

• Communicating expectations clearly
• Having a specific job description
• Identifying specific performance standards
• Specifying deadlines
• Setting goals

Video Example

(*Show the scene in* Dangerous Minds *where Michelle Pfeiffer tells her students they all start the semester with an A.*)

How might such a statement translate to a business setting?

Show video.

1 minute.

Lead discussion.

1 minute.

Answer to look for:

As long as your employees know what they must do to "keep the A," it could be very effective. The message is that the teacher (boss) believes in the students (employees) and wants to support them in doing good work.

Why is each of these important: What happens when you don't, and what happens when you do? Can you think of some examples from your own work experiences?

You may want to take some notes on Handout 11.2.

Handout 11.2.

Lead discussion; note answers on easel pad.

Answers to look for:

5 minutes.

1. Communicating expectations clearly

   When you don't: People don't know what is expected of them; they become uncomfortable and feel uncertain; they are less likely to do their jobs properly.

   When you do: People feel more confident because they are certain of what is expected; they are more likely to do their jobs properly and make fewer mistakes.

2. Having a specific job description

   When you don't: People feel less certain of what is expected; there may be more confusion in the work area because team members are uncertain about who is responsible for what.

   When you do: Work is completed more efficiently because everyone knows who is responsible for what; people are more productive because they don't need to waste time discussing who should do what.

3. Identifying specific performance standards

   When you don't: People tend to underperform when no standard has been identified, for example, how much are they expected to sell or how many items need to be filed.

   When you do: People produce more when they know more precisely what is expected; when a standard has been identified, the chances are greater that people will meet it.

4. Specifying deadlines

   When you don't: People feel less motivated when no expectation has been stated.

Outline	Presenter's Comments	Activity

When you do: People will be more motivated to complete a task when a deadline has been stated.

5. Setting goals

When you don't: When no goal has been identified, we all tend to drift along.

When you do: Having a goal is energizing and motivating. Goals give people something to look forward to; most people feel a sense of victory and satisfaction when goals are accomplished.

III-B.
Show Interest in Your Team

Skill #2 is *show interest in your team members.*

Who can describe what it is like to work in a group where people are interested in each other? What effect does it have on your productivity when people—especially the boss—are interested in you?

How would you describe what it is like to work in such an environment? *(Look for examples that illustrate that such an environment makes people more productive.)*

Ask participants to complete Handout 11.3 individually. Give yourself three minutes. Then we'll discuss it as a group.

- How do you know that someone is interested in you?
- What are the behaviors?

Answers to look for:

- Make eye contact.
- Call me by name.
- Ask my opinion.
- Smile.
- Compliment my work.
- Take my suggestions.

Ask the group for signs of lack of interest. Note these on the transparency or prepared flip chart as people call them out.

Answers to look for:

- Ignoring me
- Not knowing my name or not using it
- Not asking my opinion
- Ignoring my suggestions

Activity column:

Present information.

Lead discussion.

3 minutes.

Handout 11.3.

Complete handout.

3 minutes.

Group discussion.

List ideas on easel.

3 minutes.

Lead discussion.

3 minutes.

Outline	Presenter's Comments	Activity

- No comments on my work
- Following my suggestions, but only when heard from someone else

How do such signs make you feel? — Lead discussion.

Answers to look for:

- Discouraged
- Angry
- Less confident
- Have lower self-esteem

Do such signs encourage or discourage your level of productivity? — Lead discussion.

Answers to look for:

Such signs *discourage* productivity.

I'd like to hear about a few examples from your own work experiences. — Ask for examples.

III-C.
Create an Encouraging Environment

Skill #3 is *create an encouraging environment.* — Handout 11.4.

What does *encouraging environment* mean to you? — Lead discussion; list responses on easel.

You may wish to take notes on Handout 11.4.

Answers to look for: — 3 minutes.

- My ideas are valued.
- Creativity is encouraged.
- Risks are encouraged.
- Fun and laughter are valued.
- New ideas are rewarded.
- I feel appreciated.
- People thank me for my contributions.
- Flexibility is valued.
- I feel like part of the team.

Video Example

The next video I'd like us to consider is a scene from the movie *Dangerous Minds* where Michelle Pfeiffer announces the contest. — Show video. 1 minute. Lead discussion. 1 minute.

What are the benefits of creating such a work environment? What's in it for you? — 1 minute.

11.9

Outline	Presenter's Comments	Activity

Answers to look for:

1. Benefits to employees:

   - Contribute more ideas
   - Feel more committed
   - Look forward to coming to work
   - Are more productive
   - Have increased self-esteem

2. Benefits to manager/owner:

   - Less turnover
   - Less sabotage
   - Greater loyalty
   - Easier to find employees due to good reputation
   - Higher productivity

3 minutes.

Handout 11.5 is a list of 20 ways to create an encouraging work environment.

Handout 11.5.

Let's talk about each item on the list. I'd like to hear one or two examples of each item. If you think of new ideas, we'll add them to the list.

**III-D.
Recognize
and Reward
Good
Performance**
🕐

Skill #4 is *recognize and reward good performance.*

What do we mean by reinforcing and rewarding good performance?

Lead discussion.

3 minutes.

Answer to look for:

A reinforcer is anything that happens after a behavior that tends to increase the chances that the behavior will be repeated.

Reinforcers are things like these:

Give examples.

- Compliments
- Smiles
- Thumbs-up gesture
- Saying thank you
- Public announcement of your achievement
- Positive letter in your personnel file
- Promotion

- Time off
- Special parking space
- First choice on schedule
- Dinner with the boss
- Tickets to an event
- Extra employee discount
- Picture on the bulletin board
- Applause at a meeting

Can you think of other examples?

Ask for examples.

11.10

Outline	_Presenter's Comments_	_Activity_

We will look at more examples of rewards in a moment. First, let's consider some important guidelines about recognition.

Present information.

10 minutes.

In *1001 Ways to Reward Employees,* author Bob Nelson lists several reasons why it is more important than ever to recognize and reward employees for good performance:

1. Since managers can no longer force employees to do their jobs (as in days past), they must think of more positive and creative ways to influence and encourage them.

2. In these post-downsizing days, all workers are expected to do more work. This makes encouragement and reinforcement all the more important.

3. Everyone is working more autonomously. A positive and reinforcing work environment creates an atmosphere where people can be trusted to work independently.

4. The younger generation of workers expects to be motivated by their work.

5. Rewarding and recognizing employees can be a low-cost way to encourage people to work harder.

Lead discussion (as time allows).

Ask the group if they can think of other reasons why reinforcement is an important part of the manager's tool kit.

2 minutes.

IV. Reinforcement Guidelines

Nelson recommends a few guidelines for reinforcing and rewarding employees. You may wish to note these on Handout 11.6.

Handout 11.6.

Present information.

10 minutes.

1. Match the reward to the individual. Recognize that every person is unique and we are all motivated by different things.

2. Make certain the reward fits the achievement. A small task completed ahead of time should bring a smaller reward than finishing a major project.

3. Be specific about the performance you are recognizing; always say *why* you are recognizing or rewarding. Make certain the employee understands what is being rewarded.

For example, telling an employee "You do such great work" is a vague compliment. Ask the group what might be a more specific statement. Look for answers like "Thank you for formatting this report so well" or "I

Outline	Presenter's Comments	Activity

appreciate your staying last night until the report was finished."

4. Reward in a timely manner. Give rewards as soon as possible after the fact.

Ask the group why this is important.

Answer to look for:

The idea is to have the employee associate the reward with the behavior. This increases the chances that the behavior will be repeated.

V. Recognition Guidelines

Let's summarize the guidelines for giving recognition effectively. Handout 11.7 provides you with guidelines for translating what you've learned into action.

Please complete the handout individually; allow yourself about three minutes.

When you are finished, I'd like two or three people to share what they've written.

Why is each of the three steps outlined on the handout important?

Activity: Handout 11.7.

Complete handout.

3 minutes.

Ask 2–3 people to share.

Lead group discussion.

5 minutes.

Answers to look for:

1. *Describe the results you are recognizing. Be specific.* It's important to make certain the employee knows what behavior or accomplishment you are referring to.

2. *State your personal appreciation.* Say, "I appreciate it." Adding your personal appreciation makes the compliment feel more genuine.

3. *Encourage the person to continue producing such good work.* This increases the chances that the person will repeat the desirable behavior.

VI. Ideas for Recognizing and Rewarding Good Performance

Handout 11.8 is a list of 20 ideas for recognizing and rewarding good performance.

Let's talk about each of these and add as many more as we can think of.

1001 Ways to Reward Employees has many more ideas.

Activity: Handout 11.8.

Discuss each of the 20 ideas.

20 minutes.

VII. Conclusion

I hope you have enjoyed today's workshop. In the time remaining, I would be happy to answer any questions you may have.

Activity: Conclude the workshop.

Handout 11.1 Positive versus Negative Work Environment

Think about the places you have worked. What were the characteristics of the positive work environments? The negative?

Negative work environments

_____

_____

_____

_____

_____

_____

_____

_____

_____

_____

_____

Positive work environments

_____

_____

_____

_____

_____

_____

_____

_____

_____

_____

_____

Handout 11.2   Great Expectations

1. Why is it important to let people know what you expect of them?

    What happens when you don't? _____

    _____

    What happens when you do? _____

    _____

2. Communicating expectations clearly

    What happens when you don't? _____

    _____

    What happens when you do? _____

    _____

3. Having a specific job description

    What happens when you don't? _____

    _____

    What happens when you do? _____

    _____

4. Identifying specific performance standards

    What happens when you don't? _____

    _____

    What happens when you do? _____

    _____

5. Specifying deadlines

    What happens when you don't? _____

    _____

    What happens when you do? _____

    _____

6. Setting goals

    What happens when you don't? _____

    _____

    What happens when you do? _____

    _____

Handout 11.3   Signs of Interest

How do you know when a coworker or boss is showing appropriate professional interest in you? Make a list of as many signs as you can think of.

_____   _____

_____   _____

_____   _____

_____   _____

_____   _____

What are some signs of lack of interest?

_____   _____

_____   _____

_____   _____

How do such signs make you feel? _____

_____

Do such signs encourage or discourage your level of productivity? _____

_____

Handout 11.4   The Encouraging Work Environment

What is an encouraging work environment? List as many things as you can think of:

_____   _____

_____   _____

_____   _____

_____   _____

_____   _____

What are the benefits of creating an encouraging work environment?

Benefits to employees   Benefits to manager/owner

_____   _____

_____   _____

_____   _____

_____   _____

Handout 11.5   20 Ways to Create an Encouraging Work Environment

1. Hold meetings where you ask employees for feedback about the company and their jobs.

2. Give employees the authority to solve problems.

3. Demonstrate that you reward independent thinking.

4. Build a self-appraisal step into the performance appraisal process.

5. Tell your employees how much you appreciate them.

6. Write a note of thanks when an employee does something notable.

7. Schedule celebrations, contests, and parties.

8. Make sure employees have the information and equipment they need to do their jobs.

9. Include employees in the setting of performance goals.

10. Be visible. Get out of your office and mix with people and customers.

11. Make new employees feel welcome. Have their work space ready for them when they arrive. Show that you gave some thought to their arrival.

12. Pay attention to what is going on in employees' lives. Acknowledge milestones and express concern about difficult life situations such as illnesses, deaths, and accidents.

13. If it's possible in your business, allow employees to control their schedules.

14. Publicize and reward people for money-saving and moneymaking suggestions.

15. Look for ways to demonstrate that you trust people. Do you really need two signatures on Form X or a vice president's approval to spend $50?

16. Introduce employees when a client visits the office.

17. Post favorable customer letters and comments for everyone to see.

18. Involve employees in decisions to select and purchase new equipment.

19. When you promise to do something, follow through. When the task is complete, let the employee know.

20. Allow employees to override certain policies and alter certain procedures when it makes sense to do so and is in the customer's best interest.

Handout 11.6   Reinforcement Guidelines

1. _____

_____

2. _____

_____

3. _____

_____

4. _____

_____

5. _____

_____

Handout 11.7   Recognition Worksheet

Which of your team members would you like to recognize?

_____

What recent accomplishment do you want to reward?

_____

Following the guidelines below, what will you say to this person to recognize their accomplishment?

1. Describe the results you are recognizing. Be specific.

_____

2. State your personal appreciation.

_____

3. Encourage the person to continue producing such good work.

_____

Handout 11.8   20 Ways to Reward Employees

1. Use the person's first name when you compliment him or her.

2. Tell other people about the employee's idea or accomplishment, giving the employee credit.

3. Mention the employee's name in a report or memo where you mention his or her idea or accomplishment.

4. Name something after the employee: a room, hallway, door, award, or the like.

5. Write a letter to the employee saying thank you. Fold the letter and write "Bravo" or "Wonderful" on it.

6. Take the time to find something unusual to give to the employee as your thank-you. Make sure it conveys your message of appreciation.

7. Post employees' photos in your lobby. When people do notable things, mention it next to their photos.

8. Post thank-yous and acknowledgments on the employee bulletin boards.

9. Announce accomplishments over the public address system.

10. Mention the accomplishment to your boss and ask him or her to congratulate the employee (in addition to your own congratulations).

11. Give the employee free lunches for a week.

12. Buy lunch for the employee and the three coworkers of his or her choice.

13. Find out the person's hobby and give an appropriate gift.

14. Buy the person something for his or her child.

15. Send the person to the training seminar of his or her choice.

16. Upgrade the employee's computer or other equipment.

17. Give the person a plum assignment.

18. Mention the accomplishment in the company newsletter.

19. Make a charitable donation in the employee's name.

20. Invite the person to visit an important (relevant) management meeting.

21. Add your own ideas:

_____

_____

_____

_____

_____

_____

_____

_____

_____

Chapter 12

Managing Conflict at Work

Presentation Synopsis

Every workplace has conflicts. In some organizations, conflict is a serious problem, while in others, differences are resolved without incident. This workshop explores how people often resolve conflict at work, its effect on relationships and teams, and how we learn to manage differences as we do. Participants also learn skills for resolving and preventing conflict in the workplace.

This presentation is based, in part, on information from the following book. I recommend that you review it as you prepare your presentation.

Bower, Sharon, and Gordon Bower. *Asserting Yourself.* Reading, MA: Perseus Books, 1991.

Time Requirements

This presentation runs from 1 hour to 1½ hours, depending on the style of the presenter and the number of interactive activities used.

⏱ **Clock symbol.** This means that the information is included for a longer presentation. Omit these sections when time is limited. Another way to shorten your presentation is to make use of the lecture format. However, keep in mind that it is often harder to engage and maintain the audience's interest with pure lecture style. Unless you are an especially dynamic speaker, you will probably want to keep at least a few of the exercises to enliven the presentation.

Video examples. Showing selected scenes from popular movies is one way to make your presentation more interesting. It creates some variety and interest, stimulates discussion, and might be a way to inject some humor. Consider selecting short scenes from videos such as *Alice in Wonderland* and *Waiting to Exhale*. Suggestions for specific scenes are included in this outline, but you are encouraged to look for other examples on your own as you prepare for your presentation.

How to Use This Presentation

Possible Audiences	Whom to Contact
Chamber of Commerce	President or program chairperson
Rotary, Lions Club, and other business groups	President or program chairperson
Business networking groups, such as LEADS	President or program chairperson
Local businesses	President, owner, or manager
Women's civic and professional organizations	President or program chairperson

Sample Text for Marketing Letter, Brochure, or Postcard

_____ is offering "Managing Conflict at Work," an educational workshop, to your company or group as a community service. In this workshop, participants will explore how to manage conflict in the workplace. Through written exercises and group discussions, we will focus on common workplace situations where conflicts arise. As a result of attending this workshop, participants will learn new ways to resolve conflicts more productively and how to prevent them from happening in the first place.

_____ is a licensed _____ in private practice in _____. S/he specializes in _____ and _____. Call _____ today to schedule your group's **free** workshop. (_____) _____-_____.

Sample Text for Press Release

_____ Presents "Managing Conflict at Work" Seminar

_____ is presenting a **free** workshop on how to manage conflict in the workplace. The workshop is scheduled for _____, from _____ to _____ at _____. The workshop is limited to ____ participants and is open to the public.

According to _____, "The workplace has become increasingly stressful in recent years. Not only are workloads increasing as a result of new technology and years of downsizing, but disagreements and conflicts are more common than ever. People skills have become as important as technical skills, including the ability to manage conflict. This workshop provides an overview of some productive ways to deal with conflicts at work."

_____ is a licensed _____ in private practice in _____. S/he specializes in _____ and _____. For reservations, call _____ at (_____) _____-_____.

Exhibit 12.1   Presentation Outline

Managing Conflict at Work

Topic	Time Estimate
I. Introduction	10 minutes
A. Introduce yourself	
🕐 B. Ask group members to introduce themselves	
C. State workshop goals	
II. Kinds of workplace conflicts	3 minutes
III. Common ways of dealing with conflict	12 minutes
🕐 Video examples	
IV. The effects of conflict on work relationships	15 minutes
🕐	
V. Factors that affect conflict management	10 minutes
🕐	
VI. Conflict resolution skills	30 minutes
🕐 A. Active listening	
🕐 B. Assertive communication	
🕐 C. Deescalation skills	
VII. Conflict prevention skills	10 minutes
🕐	
VIII. Summary	1 minute
Approximate total time	**91 minutes**

Exhibit 12.2   Presentation Script

Managing Conflict at Work

Outline	Presenter's Comments	Activity
I-A. **Introduce Yourself**	My name is _____. I'm a licensed _____, with a _____. I specialize in working with _____. Many of my clients come to me with stories of conflict at work. It presents a problem for many people, and the resulting stress often spills over to their lives outside of work. When I approached _____ about presenting a workshop on managing conflict at work, his/her reaction was _____. So that is why we are here today.	Refer to your bio on the first page of the handouts.
I-B. **Group Intro** ⏱	I'd like to start things off by finding out a bit about each of you. Let's go around the room; introduce yourself and tell us what kind of work you do here at _____.	If the group is under 20 people, ask participants to introduce themselves.
I-C. **Goals**	In this workshop, we will explore conflict in the workplace. Through written exercises and group discussions, we will focus on where conflicts arise and how we typically deal with them. By the end of this workshop, you will have learned some new ways to resolve these conflicts more productively. You will also learn some ways to prevent conflicts from happening in the first place.	State goals.
II. **Kinds of Workplace Conflicts**	Let's start by identifying where conflicts happen. Think about the kinds of conflicts that happen around your workplace. What are some examples? You may wish to take notes on Handout 12.1.	Handout 12.1.
⏱	**Look for answers like these:** • Disagreements over turf (who should do what) • Disagreements over policy (how things should be done) • Conflicts of personality and style	List suggestions on easel pad. If time is short, present info as a lecture.
III. **Common Ways of Dealing with Conflict**	Now that we've identified some typical situations where conflict arises at work, let's look at some examples of ways that people deal with them. First, let's look at two examples from movies you may have seen. In *Waiting to Exhale*, Angela Bassett's character deals	

12.5

Outline	Presenter's Comments	Activity

🕐

**Video
Examples**

with conflict like this. *(Show the scene where Angela Bassett's character torches her husband's car.)*

Here is another way of dealing with conflict. In *Alice in Wonderland,* Alice and her friends respond to conflict instigated by the queen like this. *(Show scene where Alice and the playing cards agree with everything the queen says.)*

What are some other ways of dealing with conflict? You may want to list these on Handout 12.1.

Activity: List responses on Handout 12.1.

🕐

Typical answers:

- Avoid the conflict.
- Deny the conflict; wait until it goes away.
- Change the subject.
- React emotionally: Become aggressive, abusive, hysterical, or frightening.
- Find someone to blame.
- Make excuses.
- Delegate the situation to someone else.

Activity: List responses on blank easel.

If time is short, present info as a lecture.

What is wrong with these ways of responding?

Target answer:

All of these responses are nonproductive. Some of them (like Angela Bassett's) are destructive. This is why learning to manage conflict is so important.

**IV.
Effect on
Work
Relationships**

The workplace is a system of relationships. Relationships have different aspects, like trust between people and the self-esteem of the individuals involved. When conflicts are handled well, what is the effect on each of the workplace factors listed on Handout 12.1? And when conflicts are handled poorly, what is the effect?

Activity: List responses on Handout 12.1.

🕐

Look for these participant answers:

Activity: Typical answers.

If time is short, present info as a lecture.

Relationship factor	How it is affected when conflict is handled *well*	How it is affected when conflict is handled *badly*
Trust	Increases	Decreases
Teamwork	Improves	Quality declines
Morale	Improves	Declines

12.6

Self-esteem	Increases	Declines
Loyalty	Increases	Declines
Respect for boss	Increases	Declines
Productivity	Increases	Decreases
Future behavior	People feel free to express differing viewpoints	People avoid conflict and withhold their viewpoints to avoid negative consequences

Outline	Presenter's Comments	Activity
V. **Factors That Affect How People Manage Conflict**	The skills involved in managing conflict are learned behaviors. None of us is born knowing how to deal with differences of opinion or arguments or turf wars. Some of the factors that affect how we behave in the face of conflict are:	Prelist these factors on easel pad.

1. Status
2. Company style; unwritten rules
3. Gender differences
4. Behavior learned in our families
5. Behavior learned from our role models

These factors are listed on Handout 12.1. What are some examples of each of these factors? You may wish to note them on the handout.

(Activity note:) Note examples on Handout 12.1.

Offer your ideas if needed to move the discussion along:

- *Status:* People in higher-status positions usually feel freer to engage in conflict and are less likely to avoid confrontation.
- *Company style or unwritten rules:* Some companies encourage conflict; others have unwritten rules that it is to be contained or avoided.
- *Gender differences:* Males are generally encouraged to be more confrontational than females.
- *Behavior learned in families:* In some families, conflict and confrontation are a communication style. In others, conflict always remains hidden.
- *Behavior learned from role models:* People who have had a teacher or boss who modeled effective conflict resolution skills are more likely to develop these skills themselves.

(Activity note:) Encourage participants to come up with these answers.

If time is limited, present these ideas as a lecture.

Outline	Presenter's Comments	Activity
VI. **Conflict** **Resolution** **Skills**	No one is born knowing how to resolve conflicts. Conflict resolution is a set of skills that anyone can learn. These skills include: 1. Active listening 2. Assertive communication skills 3. Deescalation skills Let's spend a moment exploring each of these three skills.	
VI-A. **Active** **Listening**	You may wish to take notes on Handout 12.2. Active listening is a valuable skill for resolving conflicts because it enables you to demonstrate that you understand what another person is saying and how he or she is feeling about it. Active listening means restating, in your own words, what the other person has said. Active listening is a way of checking whether your understanding is correct. It also demonstrates that you are listening and that you are interested and concerned. These all help resolve a situation where there are conflicting points of view. Active listening responses have two components: 1. Naming the feeling that the other person is conveying 2. Stating the reason for the feeling	Handout 12.2.
Active **Listening** **Examples**	Here are some examples of active listening statements: "Sounds like you're upset about what happened at work." "You're annoyed by my lateness, aren't you?" "You sound really stumped about how to solve this problem." "It makes you angry when you find errors on Joe's paperwork." "Sounds like you're really worried about Wendy." "I get the feeling you're awfully busy right now." Active listening is not the same as agreement. It is a way of demonstrating that you intend to hear and understand another's point of view.	
Active **Listening** **Benefits**	If a person uses active listening as part of his or her communication style at work, how would that be good for resolving conflicts—that is, what are the benefits?	Handout 12.2.

12.8

Outline	Presenter's Comments	Activity

Possible responses:

1. It feels good when another person makes an effort to understand what you are thinking and feeling. It creates good feelings about the other person and makes you feel better about yourself.

2. Restating what you've heard and checking for understanding promotes better communication and produces fewer misunderstandings.

3. Responding with active listening has a calming effect in an emotional situation.

Responses to look for.

Please take a moment to try this yourself. You will find three work situations described on Handout 12.2. Write an active listening response for each one, making sure to include the two components we talked about.

Handout 12.2.

Allow 3 minutes.

Ask participants to read their responses.

1. Your company's office manager says to you, "Your payroll records are all messed up this week. I don't see how I can get your people's paychecks out because these things are so late. Who's running this place, anyway?"

   Sample response: "You sound pretty exasperated about the records."

If time is short, suggest that participants complete exercises later.

2. You are the marketing manager. The sales manager comes into your office, sits down, and buries his face in his hands. He moans, "You guys are really making things extra hard for me. How do you expect me to sell this stuff when you give me the worst marketing materials I've ever seen?"

   Sample response: "You're disgusted with the new campaign."

3. Your boss says, "You call this report finished? My 10-year-old could have done a better job."

   Sample response: "You're surprised because the report is so short."

**VI-B.
Assertive
Communication
Skills**

Another skill that will help you manage conflict effectively is to be assertive (rather than aggressive or passive) in your communication. The DESC script is a way to help you plan an assertive message. It is a tool for organizing your thoughts so you are less likely to forget what you want to say and how you want to say it. It helps minimize conflicts

Handout 12.3.

Outline	Presenter's Comments	Activity

because it is straightforward and assertive, focusing on your view of the situation.

The DESC message has four components: Describe, Express, Specify, and Consequences. This is what the four steps mean:

- *Describe* the problem or issue.
- *Express* your feelings about the situation.
- *Specify* what you want the other person to do. Be specific, including when you want the action completed.
- State the *Consequences:* Describe what you will do if the other person does not do what you are requesting.

This is an assertive alternative to saying, "Do it my way or I'll fire you" or "You need to get these reports done by noon."

Let's get some practice with this technique by completing the exercise on Handout 12.3.

Who would like to read their DESC script for the first exercise? *(If time is short, suggest that participants complete exercises later.)*

Allow 3 minutes.

Ask different people to read their answers.

Reinforce responses that are assertive; point out those that sound too threatening.

VI-C.
Deescalation

Everyone has been in an argument that has escalated. Before you know it, it's blown out of proportion. Let's think for a moment about some actions that will help you deescalate a conflict. In your experience, what actions put a stop to the defend/attack spiral? You may wish to list these on Handout 12.4.

Handout 12.4.

Typical responses:

- Stick with "I" statements; avoid "you" statements.
- Avoid name-calling and put-downs ("a reasonable person could see that . . .").
- Soften your tone.
- Take a time-out ("Let's take a break and cool down").
- Acknowledge the other person's point of view (agreement is not necessary).
- Avoid defensive or hostile body language (rolling eyes, crossing arms in front of body, tapping foot).
- Be specific and factual; avoid generalities.

If time is short, present as a lecture.

12.10

Outline	Presenter's Comments	Activity
VII. **Conflict** **Prevention** **Skills**	Now that we've talked about how to resolve a conflict, let's look at how to prevent conflicts from happening. Think of situations in your life where there don't seem to be many conflicts. What might be happening there? You may wish to note these on Handout 12.5.	Ask group to think of ways to prevent conflict. Take notes on Handout 12.5.
	Responses to look for: • Bring issues out in the open before they become problems. • Be aware of triggers and respond to them when you notice them. • Have a process for resolving conflicts. Bring it up at a meeting and get agreement on what people should do in cases of differing viewpoints. • Teach everyone conflict resolution skills and expect people to use them.	List ideas on easel. If time is short, information may be presented as a lecture.
VIII. **Conclusion**	I hope you have enjoyed today's workshop. In the time remaining, I would be happy to answer any questions you may have.	Conclude the workshop.

Handout 12.1   Handling Conflicts at Work

1. What kinds of conflicts typically occur in your workplace?

2. What are some common ways of dealing with conflict?

3. What is the effect of each of these actions on the following relationship factors?

Relationship factor	How is this factor affected when conflict is handled *well?*	How is this factor affected when conflict is handled *badly?*
Trust	_____	_____
Teamwork	_____	_____
Morale	_____	_____
Self-esteem	_____	_____
Loyalty	_____	_____
Respect	_____	_____
Productivity	_____	_____
Future behavior	_____	_____

4. These are some of the factors that affect how people manage conflict. Think of an example of each.

- Status
- Company style; unwritten rules
- Gender differences
- Behavior learned in our families
- Behavior learned from our role models

Handout 12.2   Active Listening

Active listening is a valuable skill for managing conflict because _____.

An active listening response has two components:

1. _____ and 2. _____.

Responding with active listening has these benefits:

1. _____

2. _____

3. _____

Write an active listening response to each of the following statements.

1. Your company's office manager says to you, "Your payroll records are all messed up this
    week. I don't see how I can get your people's paychecks out because these things are so late.
    Who's running this place, anyway?"

    I could say: _____

    _____

2. You are the marketing manager. The sales manager comes into your office, sits down, and
    buries his face in his hands. He moans, "You guys are really making things hard for me. How
    do you expect me to sell this stuff when you give me the worst marketing materials I've ever
    seen?"

    I could say: _____

    _____

3. Your boss says, "You call this report finished? My 10-year-old could have done a better job."

    I could say: _____

    _____

Handout 12.3   Assertive Communication Skills

The DESC Script

D _____

E _____

S _____

C _____

Situation #1:   Your assistant has just returned from lunch 30 minutes late. This is the third time in two weeks that he has done this. His lateness has caused the assistant of the manager in the next office to have to delay her lunch break, causing her to miss a doctor's appointment.

Describe: _____

Express: _____

Specify: _____

Consequences: _____

Situation #2:   You are responsible for human resources in a small company. This morning, you discovered that the manager of operations is bringing in an outside consultant to run some training workshops. He has not consulted you.

Describe: _____

Express: _____

Specify: _____

Consequences: _____

Situation #3:   You are planning a vacation in July to attend a family reunion. Your boss knows that you have been planning this event for a long time. Today you find out that your boss has made plans to be gone the same week for an educational seminar. There is a policy in your company that only one person from any department may be away from the office at a given time.

Describe: _____

Express: _____

Specify: _____

Consequences: _____

Source: Sharon and Gordon Bower, *Asserting Yourself* (Reading, MA: Perseus Books, 1991).

Handout 12.4   Conflict Deescalation

List actions that can help deescalate a conflict:

- _____
- _____
- _____
- _____
- _____
- _____
- _____
- _____
- _____
- _____
- _____
- _____
- _____

Handout 12.5   Preventing Conflict

List ways to prevent conflicts from happening:

- _____
- _____
- _____
- _____
- _____
- _____
- _____
- _____
- _____
- _____
- _____
- _____
- _____

Chapter 13

The Art of Effective Communication

Presentation Synopsis

In this workshop, participants will learn skills that will enable them to communicate with tact and diplomacy. Through written exercises and group discussion, participants will learn how to overcome barriers to communication; how to convey empathy and acceptance; how to listen, communicate assertively, give and receive constructive feedback, resolve conflicts, and manage anger constructively.

This presentation is based, in part, on information from the following books. I recommend that you review them as you prepare your presentation.

Alberti, Robert, and Michael Emmons. *Your Perfect Right,* 7th ed. Atascadero, CA: Impact, 1995.

Burley-Allen, Madelyn. *Listening: The Forgotten Skill,* 2nd ed. New York: John Wiley & Sons, 1995.

Burley-Allen, Madelyn. *Managing Assertively: A Self-Teaching Guide,* 2nd ed. New York: John Wiley & Sons, 1995.

Gordon, Thomas. *Leader Effectiveness Training.* New York: Bantam Doubleday Dell, 1986.

McKay, Matthew, Peter Rogers, and Judith McKay. *When Anger Hurts: Quieting the Storm Within.* Oakland, CA: New Harbinger, 1989.

Rosellini, Gayle, and Mark Worden. *Of Course You're Angry,* 2nd ed. Center City, MN: Hazelden Foundation, 1997.

Tavris, Carol. *Anger: The Misunderstood Emotion.* New York: Touchstone, 1989.

Time Requirements

This presentation runs from 1½ hours to 2 hours, depending on the style of the presenter and the number of interactive activities used.

🕐 **Clock symbol.** This means that the information is included for a longer seminar or workshop. Omit these sections for a shorter presentation. If time is limited, another way to shorten your presentation is to share the information in lecture format. However, keep in mind that it is often harder to engage and maintain the audience's interest with pure lecture style. Unless you are a particularly dynamic speaker, you will probably want to keep at least a few of the exercises to enliven the presentation.

How to Use This Presentation

Possible Audiences

Civic and professional organizations
Businesspeople

Adult education groups at churches and
synagogues

Whom to Contact

Director of educational programs
Company presidents, human resources managers,
or other executives; Chamber of Commerce,
Rotary, and similar business groups
Director of adult education programs

Sample Text for Marketing Letter, Brochure, or Postcard

Most of us have spent considerable time and expense developing our technical skills in order to succeed in the workplace. Our interpersonal skills, however, often need some improvement. In this workshop, participants will learn skills that will enable them to communicate with tact and diplomacy. Through written exercises and group discussion, participants will learn how to overcome barriers to communication; how to convey empathy and acceptance; how to listen, communicate assertively, give and receive constructive feedback, resolve conflicts, and manage anger constructively.

_____ is offering this educational and motivational seminar to your group as a community service. _____ is a licensed _____ in private practice in _____. S/he specializes in _____ and _____. Call today to schedule your group's **free** workshop. (_____) _____-_____.

Sample Text for Press Release

_____ Presents "The Art of Effective Communication"

_____ is presenting a **free** workshop on how to communicate more effectively at work. The workshop is scheduled for _____, from _____ to _____ at _____. It is designed for anyone who works with other people and is limited to ____ participants. It is open to members of _____ and the public.

According to _____, "Most of us have spent considerable time and expense developing our technical skills in order to succeed in the workplace. Our interpersonal skills, however, often need some improvement. In this workshop, participants will learn skills that will enable them to overcome barriers to communication; how to convey empathy and acceptance; how to listen, communicate assertively, give and receive constructive feedback, resolve conflicts, and manage anger constructively."

_____ is a licensed _____ in private practice in _____. S/he specializes in _____ and _____. For reservations, call _____ at (_____) _____-_____.

Exhibit 13.1   Presentation Outline

The Art of Effective Communication

Topic Time Estimate

I. **Introduction** 2–12 minutes
   A. Introduce yourself
   🕐 B. Ask group members to introduce themselves
   C. State workshop goals

II. **Importance of communication** 21–37 minutes
   🕐 A. Barriers to communication
   🕐 B. 12 communication roadblocks
   C. Why roadblocks hinder communication

III. **Empathy and acceptance** 5 minutes

IV. **Listening skills** 20 minutes
   A. Open-ended questions
   B. Summary statements
   C. Neutral questions and phrases
   D. Listening skills: practice exercises

V. **Assertive communication** 5 minutes

VI. **Giving and receiving constructive feedback** 18 minutes
   A. You-messages
   B. I-messages

VII. **Resolving conflicts** 10 minutes

VIII. **Managing anger** 15 minutes
   A. Time-out
   B. Make a contract
   C. Ask questions
   D. Positive statements
   E. Prepared response

IX. **Conclusion**

Approximate total time **96–122 minutes**

```
┌─────────────────────────────────────────────────────────────────────┐
│                                                                       │
│              Exhibit 13.2    Presentation Script                      │
│                                                                       │
└─────────────────────────────────────────────────────────────────────┘
```

The Art of Effective Communication

Outline	Presenter's Comments	Activity
I-A. **Introduce Yourself**	My name is _____. I'm a licensed _____, with a _____. I specialize in working with _____, and became interested in why so many people seem to have trouble communicating with others at work. I started noticing this _____ ago, when _____.	Refer to your bio on the first page of the handouts. 1 minute.
I-B. **Group Intro** ☉	I'd like to start things off today by finding out a bit about each of you. Let's go around the room and have each person tell us: • Your name • What types of communication problems you have experienced at work	If the group is under 20 people, ask participants to introduce themselves. 10 minutes.
I-C. **Goals**	Today's presentation is designed for anyone who works with other people. This is what you will learn: • How to overcome barriers to communication • How to convey empathy and acceptance • Listening skills • Assertive communication skills • How to give and receive constructive feedback • Some tips for resolving conflicts • Ways to manage anger constructively	State goals. 1 minute.
II. **Importance of Communication**	Any human resources manager will tell you that one of the biggest problems they see when managers need help is poor communication skill. People get into trouble in their work relationships because they have not developed their ability to listen and communicate.	Introduce subject. 1 minute.
II-A. **Barriers to Communication** ☉	Let's begin our workshop with this important subject. Why do people not communicate effectively? What do you think the barriers are? **Examples to provide if none are offered:** • Not knowing how to communicate properly • Not taking the time to think through what you want to say	Ask question. 1–2 minutes. If time is limited, present this information as a lecture.

13.6

Outline	Presenter's Comments	Activity

- Not taking the time to anticipate what your coworker might be thinking and feeling
- Fear of revealing too much of yourself
- Fear of another person's anger
- Not wanting to hurt another person's feelings

II-B.
12
Communication
Roadblocks
🕐

In his classic book *Leader Effectiveness Training,* author Thomas Gordon lists 12 ways people often communicate—ineffectively. These are very common ways of attempting to gain control and solve a problem, but they are in fact roadblocks to effective communication. These 12 roadblocks are listed on Handout 13.1.

Handout 13.1.

Let's look at each roadblock. I'll give you one example of each and ask you to think of other examples. You may want to take notes on the handout.

Read roadblocks.

1. Ordering, directing, commanding

   Example: You must be home by 5 P.M.

Give examples.

If time allows, ask for other examples.

10–25 minutes.

2. Warning, admonishing, threatening

   Example: You had better do it, or I'll be furious.

3. Moralizing, preaching, imploring

   Example: You should do this.

4. Advising, giving suggestions or solutions

   Example: I really think you should do it this way.

5. Persuading with logic, lecturing, arguing

   Example: Your way makes no sense at all.

6. Judging, criticizing, disagreeing, blaming

   Example: I can't believe you wore that.

7. Praising, agreeing, evaluating positively, buttering up

   Example: You are such a competent person.

8. Name-calling, ridiculing, shaming

   Example: You have no sense of direction.

9. Interpreting, analyzing, diagnosing

   Example: You're saying this because you're jealous.

10. Reassuring, sympathizing, consoling, supporting

    Example: You'll feel better tomorrow.

13.7

Outline	Presenter's Comments	Activity

11. Probing, questioning, interrogating

    Example: How do you know it will work?

12. Distracting, diverting, kidding

    Example: You think that's bad? Wait till I tell you about *my* operation.

**II-C.
Why
Roadblocks
Hinder
Communication**

What's the *problem* with these messages?

Activity: Ask question. 1 minute.

Answer to look for:

They all convey the desire to change rather than accept the other person. They all communicate a desire for the other person to think, feel, or behave differently. This means they communicate *lack of acceptance.*

A climate of lack of acceptance is not conducive to personal growth and emotional well-being.

Activity: Present information. 8 minutes.

When people feel judged, threatened, put down, or analyzed, they feel defensive and resistant to change. Such a climate also inhibits self-expression and self-exploration—both of which are necessary for solving one's own problems.

Finally, these statements take the responsibility for change away from the owner of the problem and place it in the hands of the speaker. It is important to keep the accountability focused on the person who owns the problem.

**III.
Empathy and
Acceptance**

Thomas Gordon says that at least two ingredients are necessary for any relationship to be healthy: empathy and acceptance.

Activity: Present information. 5 minutes.

How would you define empathy?

Activity: Ask question.

Answer to look for:

Empathy is the capacity to put yourself in others' shoes and understand how they view their reality, how they feel about things.

Demonstrating empathy and acceptance is critical to maintaining a strong relationship with anyone in your life, both at work or at home. Now we are going to look at some communication skills that enable you to create a climate of empathy, acceptance, and understanding in your relationships.

Outline	Presenter's Comments	Activity
IV. **Listening** **Skills**	Let's begin with listening skills. They are summarized on Handout 13.2. These skills enable you to demonstrate that you are interested in what the other person has to say. You will also learn to demonstrate that you are hearing and understanding the other person.	Handout 13.2. Present information. 10 minutes.
IV-A. **Open-ended** **Questions**	Open-ended questions begin with *what, why, how do,* or *tell me.* • These questions get the other person to open up and elaborate on the topic. • Asking these kinds of questions gets the other person involved by giving him or her a chance to tell what he or she thinks or knows. • These questions are designed to encourage your coworker to talk. • They are useful when the other person is silent or reluctant to elaborate. • They are also useful in dealing with negative emotions (such as anger or fear), since they help encourage the other person to vent feelings.	
IV-B. **Summary** **Statements**	Summary statements sum up what you hear your coworker saying. • A summary statement enhances the other person's self-esteem by showing that you were listening carefully. • It also helps you focus on facts, not emotions. • It helps the other person clarify his or her own thinking by hearing your summary. • Summary statements also help you deal with multiple disagreements so you can deal with them one by one. • They help eliminate confusion by focusing on the relevant facts. • Summary statements also help you separate the important issues from the trivial.	
IV-C. **Neutral** **Questions** **and Phrases**	Neutral questions and phrases get the other person to open up and elaborate on the topic you are discussing. • These questions are more focused than open-ended questions. • They help the other person understand what you are interested in hearing more about. • They further communication because they help you gain more information.	

Outline	Presenter's Comments	Activity
	• When you ask these kinds of questions, you demonstrate to the other person that you are interested and that you are listening.	
IV-D. **Listening Skills:** **Practice Exercises**	Now I'd like you to practice using these listening skills by completing the exercises in Handout 13.2. Take five minutes to complete the exercise. Then we will go over it as a group and discuss a few people's responses.	Handout 13.2. Complete exercise. Discuss answers as a group. 10 minutes.
	Let's see what a few of you wrote for each item in this exercise. There is no one right answer or type of answer. The idea here is to make certain that you understand how these communication skills are used.	
V. **Assertive Communication**	Assertive communication is a constructive way of expressing feelings and opinions.	Handout 13.3. Complete exercises. Discuss answers. 5 minutes.
	Let's read through Handout 13.3 together. The first section defines assertive behavior and contrasts it with passive and aggressive behavior.	
	Next, please complete the exercises on this handout. When you are finished, we will discuss them.	

Answers:

Exercise #1: Aggressive

Exercise #2: Passive

Exercise #3: Assertive

Outline	Presenter's Comments	Activity
VI. **Giving and Receiving Constructive Feedback**	Giving and receiving constructive feedback is another important communication skill. One effective way to do this is with the I-message.	Handout 13.4. 8 minutes.
	I am going to introduce this skill to you by describing what it doesn't sound like. Please refer to Handout 13.4.	
VI-A. **You-Messages**	How do you think you would feel if a coworker spoke to you like this?	Read examples of you-messages.

Answer to look for:

Bad, talked down to, disrespected, and so on.

	If you want to demonstrate to another person that you respect and esteem him or her, try speaking with I-messages instead. Let's look at the examples on this handout.	Read examples.

Outline	Presenter's Comments	Activity
VI-B. **I-Messages**	Why do you think I-messages would be a more effective way of communicating than you-messages?	Ask question.

Answers to look for:

1. When you start your statement with "I," you are taking responsibility for the statement.

2. The I-message sounds less blameful and less negative than the you-message.

	Please complete the practice exercises on Handout 13.4. Take about five minutes.	Handout 13.4. Complete exercises.
	Who would like to share their responses with the rest of us? Keep in mind that there are no correct answers, but make certain that you understand the components of the I-message.	Discuss answers. 10 minutes.
VII. **Resolving** **Conflicts**	Resolving conflict is a critical skill in the workplace. Handout 13.5 outlines 12 steps for successfully managing conflict.	Handout 13.5.
	Let's read through the steps of the process together.	Read through steps.
	• What would happen if you used a process like this most of the time when you had a conflict at work?	Ask discussion questions.
	• What are the greatest barriers to using a process like this?	10 minutes.

Answers to expect:

Time, impatience

	How do you think you will respond to these barriers?	Ask question.
VIII. **Managing** **Anger**	Managing angry feelings—yours and others'—is another important skill that will help you build successful work relationships.	Handout 13.6. Complete and discuss the practice exercises together.
	Handout 13.6 details a few constructive responses to situations where you feel angry.	5 minutes.
	Let's look at each example on the handout.	Handout 13.7.
	Now that we've talked about what anger is and how it is often an automatic response to a trigger, let's spend a few moments on how to interrupt the process of an angry reaction.	
	Suggest that participants take notes on Handout 13.7.	

Outline	Presenter's Comments	Activity
VIII-A. **Time-out**	1. Time-out is a very effective technique for breaking the sequence of behavior that leads to a blowup. It works best if it is discussed ahead of time and both people agree to use it. Here is how it works: Either person in an interaction can initiate time-out. One person makes the time-out gesture like a referee in a football game: Just make a "T" sign with your hands. The other person is obligated to return the gesture and stop talking. This technique does not involve making any further statement, such as "I am getting upset." The only thing that might be said is "Time out." The T-sign is a signal that it is best to separate for a while to cool off; an hour works best. It is important to return after the hour.	Present information. 10 minutes.
VIII-B. **Make a** **Contract**	2. Make a time-out contract: To emphasize your commitment to changing your anger behavior, you and the other person may even decide to write and sign a contract outlining the details of your time-out agreement. This is especially helpful if anger has become a significant threat to the working relationship.	
VIII-C. **Ask** **Questions**	3. Ask questions: If anger is a response to personal pain, it may make sense to ask the other person, "What's hurting?"	
VIII-D. **Positive** **Statements**	4. It may be helpful to memorize a few positive statements to say to yourself when your anger is being triggered. These statements can remind you that you can choose your behavior instead of reacting in a knee-jerk manner. For example: "I can take care of my own needs." "His needs are just as important as mine." "I am able to make good choices."	
VIII-E. **Prepared** **Response**	5. Be prepared with a response. Here are a few statements and questions that will help deescalate anger. Commit one or two to memory and use them when a situation is becoming heated: • What's bothering me is . . . • And what I think I'd like is . . . • What would you suggest we do about this?	

Outline	*Presenter's Comments*	*Activity*

- If this continues like this, I'll have to do X to take care of myself.
- What do you need now?
- So what you want is . . .
- It feels like we're getting angry about this. I want to stop and cool down for a minute.

What other ideas do you have for deescalating anger? — Ask question.

IX. Conclusion I hope you have enjoyed today's workshop. In the time remaining, I would be happy to answer any questions you may have. — Conclude the workshop.

Handout 13.1 12 Communication Roadblocks

1. Ordering, directing, commanding

   _____

2. Warning, admonishing, threatening

   _____

3. Moralizing, preaching, imploring

   _____

4. Advising, giving suggestions or solutions

   _____

5. Persuading with logic, lecturing, arguing

   _____

6. Judging, criticizing, disagreeing, blaming

   _____

7. Praising, agreeing, evaluating positively, buttering up

   _____

8. Name-calling, ridiculing, shaming

   _____

9. Interpreting, analyzing, diagnosing

   _____

10. Reassuring, sympathizing, consoling, supporting

    _____

11. Probing, questioning, interrogating

    _____

12. Distracting, diverting, kidding

    _____

Source: Thomas Gordon, *Leader Effectiveness Training* (New York: Bantam Doubleday Dell, 1986).

Handout 13.2   Listening Skills

1. Open-Ended Questions

Ask open-ended questions to encourage your coworker to talk to you and share his or her feelings.

Definition: Open-ended questions cannot be answered "yes" or "no." They are phrased to encourage the other person to give a broad response to your question.

Examples: "How do you feel about what she said?"

"Tell me all about this new project."

"What do you think about the new offices?"

Other benefits of asking open-ended questions:

_____

_____

2. Summary Statements

Summarize what you hear the other person saying. A summary statement enhances the other person's self-esteem by showing that you were listening carefully.

Definition: A statement that summarizes the facts you gathered.

Examples: "So you're saying you want to go to the factory before you write those orders. Then you want to go over them with me.

"You're saying that you tried your best, but it was beyond your control."

Other benefits of making summary statements:

_____

_____

3. Neutral Questions and Phrases

Definition: Questions that encourage the other person to elaborate on some aspect of the topic being discussed.

Examples: "Give me some more reasons why we should buy the computer now rather than in January."

"Tell me more about why you want to take this job."

Other benefits of neutral questions and phrases:

_____

_____

Listening Skills: Practice Exercises

Directions: Choose a listening skill for each situation. Write an example of what you could say to the other person to validate his or her feelings and encourage further expression of emotion.

1. Your coworker returns from an important business trip. He is very quiet. When you ask him how the trip went, he shrugs his shoulders and says, "Okay."

   Which listening skill
   would work best here? _____

   I would say: _____

   _____

2. "I really wish we didn't have to go to that conference next week. I know I have to, but I wish I could get out of it somehow. I don't like traveling, I hate being away from my family, and I resent having to spend time kissing up to those vendors!"

   Which listening skill
   would work best here? _____

   I would say: _____

   _____

3. "I wish I could just stay home and garden today," your coworker says.

   Which listening skill would work best here?

   I would say: _____

   _____

4. You are 20 minutes late to pick up your coworker for a meeting. There was no way you could let him know you were going to be late. When you arrive, he opens the car door and glares at you. He growls, "I thought we agreed that you'd be on time for once!"

   Which listening skill
   would work best here? _____

   I would say: _____

   _____

5. Your business partner wants to stay in your present office space, which you have outgrown. You want to look for a bigger place. She says, "It makes me so nervous to make such a big commitment! And what if we don't like it in the new place? I think we should just stay where we are."

   Which listening skill
   would work best here? _____

   I would say: _____

   _____

Assertive behavior enables you to:

- Act in your own best interests.
- Stand up for yourself without becoming anxious.
- Express your honest feelings.
- Assert your personal rights, without denying the rights of others.

Assertive behavior is:

- Self-expressive
- Honest
- Direct
- Self-enhancing
- Not harmful to others
- Appropriate to the person and situation rather than universal
- Socially responsible
- A combination of learned skills, not an inborn trait

Assertive behavior includes both *what* you say and *how* you say it.

Assertive, Aggressive, or Passive?

Read each of the following conversations and decide whether each illustrates aggressive, passive, or assertive behavior.

Example #1

ELLEN: Listen, I've got a big problem with what you did. I've had it with these stupid mistakes on these reports. Either you stop screwing up or you're finished!

JACK: Give me a break, Ellen. You know it wasn't my fault.

ELLEN: Yeah, right! All I ever hear from you is excuses!

JACK: Those aren't excuses, Ellen. They're facts.

ELLEN: When are you going to do it the way I told you to do it?

Ellen's behavior is: _____

Example #2

ELLEN: Jack, I wish you'd be more careful with the reports.

JACK: I told you, Ellen, it wasn't my fault.

ELLEN: Oh, I'm sorry. You're right.

Ellen's behavior is: _____

Example #3

ELLEN: Jack, these mistakes created a big problem for me. I ended up making a bad decision based on that report and now I feel very embarrassed.

JACK: I told you, Ellen, it wasn't my fault.

ELLEN: I know you've had some problems, Jack. But I have to ask you to double-check your numbers in the future, and make sure you list all of your work. Will you agree to do that?

JACK: Sure, I think I can agree to that.

ELLEN: Thanks, Jack. I hope this solves the problem.

Ellen's behavior is: _____

Source: Robert Alberti and Michael Emmons, *Your Perfect Right,* 7th ed. (Atascadero, CA: Impact, 1995).

You-Messages

Examples: "You need to be here by 9:00 A.M. tomorrow."

"You shouldn't do that."

"You should call me from the airport and tell me when you'll be back in the office."

"You are rude to my friends."

"Here is what you ought to do."

Why they damage relationships:

_____

_____

I-messages

Components: Behavior + Feelings + Effects

Examples: "When I'm not kept informed about what's going on, I get worried and start imagining that you're having problems that are not getting solved."

"When you don't call from the airport, I feel left in the dark and don't know what to say to Alex when he asks where you are."

"When I heard that you'd planned a weekend up north, I was surprised that you hadn't asked me for the time off, so I could be sure to arrange for someone to cover your hours."

Why they are more effective than you-messages:

_____

_____

Practice Exercises

Convert these you-messages to I-messages and see how much more positive they sound:

1. "You need to come in by 9:00 A.M. tomorrow."

    I-message: _____

    _____

2. "You are rude to my friends."

    I-message: _____

    _____

3. "Here is what you ought to do."

   I-message: _____

   _____

4. "You should have chosen something more appropriate to wear."

   I-message: _____

   _____

Handout 13.5   Managing Conflict

1. Agree on the rules ahead of time.

2. Choose a time when you and the other person feel calm.

3. Call a time-out if emotions begin to escalate. Set a time to return.

4. One person has the floor at a time. Set a timer if you wish.

5. Alternate the roles of speaker and listener as you each present your point of view.

    Speaker: State how you see the problem.

    Focus on the problem, not the person.

    Use I-messages.

    Listener: Ask questions to clarify and further your understanding.

    Summarize the issues as you understand them.

    Listen and avoid judging what the speaker says.

6. Each person states his or her point of view.

7. When both coworkers have stated their points of view, come to agreement on what the problems are.

8. Brainstorm solutions.

9. State what action each of you would be willing to take.

10. Agree on a solution that fits both of your needs.

11. Agree on an action plan.

12. Follow through and take action.

Handout 13.6   A Better Response

Many of our angry responses occur because we simply don't take the time to think ahead and plan an alternative. Take a moment to consider these three constructive alternatives to anger.

1. Set limits.

Example: You are angry that your coworkers left a mess in the conference room. They left food and papers all over the table and knew that you had an important meeting scheduled to begin as soon as they finished theirs. You feel yourself about to blow up.

Sample response: (a) Acknowledge to yourself that your anger is your response. (b) Set limits. State your requests or demands clearly.

You could say to your coworker: "I am very disappointed in the way the conference room looks. It is not acceptable for you to leave it in this condition. I want you to clean it right now. In the future, I will remind you when I have a meeting right after yours."

Try another example: Last week, your coworker borrowed a tape recorder from your office for a presentation. You told her that you needed it back no later than yesterday, but she still hasn't returned it. You stop by her office to remind her to bring it home.

What could you say to your coworker?

(a) _____

(b) _____

2. Don't wait for other people to meet your needs.

Example: You are angry that your coworker hasn't cleared off his desk in two weeks. You are starting to be embarrassed by how the office looks. He doesn't seem to be too concerned about it, but he is too busy at work to do much besides his own work.

Sample response: (a) Acknowledge to yourself that your anger is your response. (b) Get your needs met some other way.

You could say to your coworker: "I am embarrassed by the way the office looks. I understand that you don't have time to clean your desk off. I'm going to ask the housekeeping staff to take care of it for you. That way it won't bother me, and I won't have to feel angry at you."

Try another example: You need to buy a baby gift for a coworker. You were going to get it yourself, but your assistant insisted that she has the time and has something special in mind. That was a month ago. The coworker is coming back to work soon and you feel embarrassed that you haven't sent a gift yet.

What could you say to your assistant?

(a) _____

(b) _____

3. Be assertive.

Example: You told your coworker at the beginning of the summer that you wanted to have a meeting to plan some important projects for the holiday season. She agreed that it was a good idea, but whenever you ask her to choose a date, she is always too busy. You feel angry because these projects mean a lot to you. Meanwhile, it's almost August.

Sample response: (a) Acknowledge to yourself that your anger is your response. (b) Negotiate assertively.

You could say to your coworker: "I am going to plan these projects next Tuesday. I want to get it done before the summer is over and I hope you'll be able to meet with me. Don't you agree that it's important?"

Try another example: You want to upgrade the computer in your small office. It is too slow and crashes almost every day now. You've brought it up to your partner before, and he seems to agree that it needs to be done. You are both concerned about the cost, but you realize it is necessary.

What could you say to your partner?

(a) _____

(b) _____

Handout 13.7 Five Ways to Interrupt Anger

The following five techniques may be helpful in stopping the spiral of anger.

1. Time-out

   _____

   _____

2. Make a contract

   _____

   _____

3. Ask questions

   _____

   _____

4. Positive statements

   _____

   _____

5. Be prepared with a response

   _____

   _____

About the Disk

Introduction

The forms on the enclosed disk are saved in Microsoft Word for Windows version 7.0. In order to use the forms, you will need to have word processing software capable of reading Microsoft Word for Windows version 7.0 files.

System Requirements

- IBM PC or compatible computer
- 3.5-inch floppy disk drive
- Windows 95 or later
- Microsoft Word for Windows version 7.0 (including the Microsoft converter*) or later or other word processing software capable of reading Microsoft Word for Windows 7.0 files

Note: Many popular word processing programs are capable of reading Microsoft Word for Windows 7.0 files. However, users should be aware that a slight amount of formatting might be lost when using a program other than Microsoft Word. If your word processor cannot read Microsoft Word for Windows 7.0 files, unformatted text files have been provided in the TXT directory on the floppy disk.

How to Install the Files onto Your Computer

To install the files, follow these instructions:

1. Insert the enclosed disk into the floppy disk drive of your computer.
2. From the Start menu, choose **Run**.
3. Type **A:\SETUP** and press **OK**.
4. The opening screen of the installation program will appear. Press **OK** to continue.
5. The default destination directory is C:\WORK. If you wish to change the default destination, you may do so now.
6. Press **OK** to continue. The installation program will copy all files to your hard drive in the C:\WORK or user-designated directory.

---

* Word 7.0 needs the Microsoft converter file installed in order to view and edit all enclosed files. If you have trouble viewing the files, download the free converter from the Microsoft web site. The URL for the converter is http://officeupdate.microsoft.com/downloadDetails/wd97cnv.htm.

Microsoft also has a viewer that can be downloaded, which allows you to view but not edit documents. This viewer can be downloaded at http://officeupdate.microsoft.com/downloadDetails/wd97vwr32.htm.

Using the Files

LOADING FILES

To use the word processing files, launch your word processing program. Select **File, Open** from the pull-down menu. Select the appropriate drive and directory. If you installed the files to the default directory, the files will be located in the C:\WORK directory. A list of files should appear. If you do not see a list of files in the directory, you need to select **WORD DOCUMENT(*.DOC)** under **Files of Type.** Double-click on the file you want to open. Edit the file according to your needs.

PRINTING FILES

If you want to print the files, select **File, Print** from the pull-down menu.

SAVING FILES

When you have finished editing a file, you should save it under a new file name by selecting **File, Save As** from the pull-down menu.

User Assistance

If you need assistance with installation or if you have a damaged disk, please contact Wiley Technical Support at:

Phone:	(212) 850-6753
Fax:	(212) 850-6800 (Attention: Wiley Technical Support)
E-mail:	techhelp@wiley.com

To place additional orders or to request information about other Wiley products, please call (800) 225-5945.

Disk Contents

Exhibit 1.1	A Sample Brochure	E01.01.DOC
Exhibit 1.2	A Sample Press Release	E01.02.DOC
Exhibit 1.3	A Sample Workshop Evaluation Form	E01.03.DOC
Exhibit 2.1	Types of Seating Arrangements	E02.01.DOC
Exhibit 4.1	Presentation Outline	E04.01.DOC
Exhibit 4.2	Presentation Script	E04.02.DOC
Handout 4.1	What Is Emotional Intelligence?	H04.01.DOC
Handout 4.2	The Emotional Competence Framework	H04.02.DOC
Handout 4.3	Emotional Intelligence Quiz	H04.03.DOC
Handout 4.4	Communication Skills	H04.04.DOC
Handout 4.5	Listening Behavior	H04.05.DOC
Exhibit 5.1	Presentation Outline	E05.01.DOC
Exhibit 5.2	Presentation Script	E05.02.DOC
Handout 5.1	What Is Constructive Performance Feedback?	H05.01.DOC
Handout 5.2	Giving Constructive Performance Feedback	H05.02.DOC
Handout 5.3	Other Considerations	H05.03.DOC
Handout 5.4	Practice Exercises	H05.04.DOC
Handout 5.5	Role-Play Exercises	H05.05.DOC

Exhibit 6.1	Presentation Outline	E06.01.DOC
Exhibit 6.2	Presentation Script	E06.02.DOC
Handout 6.1	What Is Your Definition of Success?	H06.01.DOC
Handout 6.2	Balance Points	H06.02.DOC
Handout 6.3	The 80/20 Rule (Pareto Principle)	H06.03.DOC
Handout 6.4	Your Top 20	H06.04.DOC
Handout 6.5	Great Relationships: Five Ingredients	H06.05.DOC
Handout 6.6	Seven Daily Habits	H06.06.DOC
Handout 6.7	How Do You Know If You Are a Workaholic?	H06.07.DOC
Exhibit 7.1	Presentation Outline	E07.01.DOC
Exhibit 7.2	Presentation Script	E07.02.DOC
Handout 7.1	Career Crash	H07.01.DOC
Handout 7.2	The Career Crash Recovery Exercise	H07.02.DOC
Exhibit 8.1	Presentation Outline	E08.01.DOC
Exhibit 8.2	Presentation Script	E08.02.DOC
Handout 8.1	Does Your Company Need Family Therapy?	H08.01.DOC
Exhibit 9.1	Presentation Outline	E09.01.DOC
Exhibit 9.2	Presentation Script	E09.02.DOC
Handout 9.1	Goals	H09.01.DOC
Handout 9.2	How to Write Goals That Motivate	H09.02.DOC
Handout 9.3	How to Write Effective Goals	H09.03.DOC
Handout 9.4	The Achievement Process	H09.04.DOC
Handout 9.5	High-Payoff Planning	H09.05.DOC
Handout 9.6	Strategies for High- and Low-Payoff Activities	H09.06.DOC
Handout 9.7	Identify Your High-Payoff Targets	H09.07.DOC
Handout 9.8	Minimize Low-Payoff Tasks	H09.08.DOC
Handout 9.9	Force-Field Analysis	H09.09.DOC
Handout 9.10	Seven Common Obstacles	H09.10.DOC
Handout 9.11	Your Action Plan	H09.11.DOC
Exhibit 10.1	Presentation Outline	E10.01.DOC
Exhibit 10.2	Presentation Script	E10.02.DOC
Handout 10.1	Sources of Stress	H10.01.DOC
Handout 10.2	Life Events	H10.02.DOC
Handout 10.3	Strategies for Managing Stress	H10.03.DOC
Handout 10.4	Manage Stress and Maximize Well-Being	H10.04.DOC
Exhibit 11.1	Presentation Outline	E11.01.DOC
Exhibit 11.2	Presentation Script	E11.02.DOC
Handout 11.1	Positive versus Negative Work Environment	H11.01.DOC
Handout 11.2	Great Expectations	H11.02.DOC
Handout 11.3	Signs of Interest	H11.03.DOC
Handout 11.4	The Encouraging Work Environment	H11.04.DOC
Handout 11.5	20 Ways to Create an Encouraging Work Environment	H11.05.DOC
Handout 11.6	Reinforcement Guidelines	H11.06.DOC
Handout 11.7	Recognition Worksheet	H11.07.DOC
Handout 11.8	20 Ways to Reward Employees	H11.08.DOC
Exhibit 12.1	Presentation Outline	E12.01.DOC
Exhibit 12.2	Presentation Script	E12.02.DOC

About the Disk

For information about the disk see the "About the Disk" section on page D.1.